S0-CUN-234

3 2528 10406 6537

WITHDRAWN
USJ Library

Robert L. Menz, DMin

A Pastoral Counselor's Model for Wellness in the Workplace
Psychergonomics

Pre-publication
REVIEWS,
COMMENTARIES,
EVALUATIONS . . .

"**A**lthough ergonomics has become a popular concept in workplace safety and comfort, the 'psyche' has generally been neglected. Dr. Menz has filled the gap with a creative expansion of ergonomics to 'psychergonomics,' which considers the well-being of the mind, body, and spirit. As an experienced health care chaplain and a certified pastoral counselor, Menz speaks with clarity and understanding about these roles in workplace ministry. From the perspective of his own workplace ministry, Menz addresses pressing issues such as violence and community. In clarifying what he means by psychergonomics, he gives a helpful overview of the major mental and emotional disorders that are common in workplace settings, and he provides a comprehensive summary of the concept and practice of wellness. Adding his own experiences, the author includes well-documented references on the studies and literature related to mind-body-spirit integration. The appendix contains very useful summaries of the symptoms of and responses to specific human problems, including substance abuse, depression, anger, conflict, and other common concerns.

Bob Menz opens a door on a vital context for a meaningful, creative, and often overlooked locus of pastoral care and counseling ministry. This book is an excellent portrayal of the possibilities and needs for qualified chaplains and pastoral counselors in the workplace, and I recommend it highly."

C. Roy Woodruff, PhD
Executive Director,
American Association
of Pastoral Counselors

More pre-publication
REVIEWS, COMMENTARIES, EVALUATIONS . . .

"*A Pastoral Counselor's Model for Wellness in the Workplace* provides valuable insight into the complicated human equation. Dr. Menz has captured much of the interconnectedness of body, mind, and spirit in an easy to comprehend, straightforward manner.

Chaplains, pastoral counselors, human resources professionals, and health care workers will appreciate the insights of chapters four and five in which Dr. Menz ties thoughts, emotions, faith, reactions, and personality characteristics to wellness or the absence thereof. In writing this useful, informative book, Dr. Menz has done us all a great service."

Roger E. Grinstead, MA
Senior Vice President,
Copeland Corporation

"This book is a must-read for chaplains and pastoral counselors wishing to understand and apply holistic health care to troubled employees, whether they be nurses, physicians, other health care workers, or workers in other industries. This book is filled with practical ideas and tools to help clergy care for the physical, mental, and spiritual needs of employees in the workplace."

Harold G. Koenig, MD
Associate Professor of Psychiatry,
Duke University Medical Center;
Author, *Chronic Pain: Biomedical and Spiritual Approaches*

The Haworth Pastoral Press®
An Imprint of The Haworth Press, Inc.
New York • London • Oxford

NOTES FOR PROFESSIONAL LIBRARIANS AND LIBRARY USERS

This is an original book title published by The Haworth Pastoral Press®, an imprint of The Haworth Press, Inc. Unless otherwise noted in specific chapters with attribution, materials in this book have not been previously published elsewhere in any format or language.

CONSERVATION AND PRESERVATION NOTES

All books published by The Haworth Press, Inc. and its imprints are printed on certified pH neutral, acid free book grade paper. This paper meets the minimum requirements of American National Standard for Information Sciences-Permanence of Paper for Printed Material, ANSI Z39.48-1984.

A Pastoral Counselor's Model for Wellness in the Workplace
Psychergonomics

A Pastoral Counselor's Model for Wellness in the Workplace
Psychergonomics

Robert L. Menz, DMin

The Haworth Pastoral Press®
An Imprint of The Haworth Press, Inc.
New York • London • Oxford

Published by

The Haworth Pastoral Press®, an imprint of The Haworth Press, Inc., 10 Alice Street, Binghamton, NY 13904-1580.

© 2003 by The Haworth Press, Inc. All rights reserved. No part of this work may be reproduced or utilized in any form or by any means, electronic or mechanical, including photocopying, microfilm, and recording, or by any information storage and retrieval system, without permission in writing from the publisher. Printed in the United States of America.

PUBLISHER'S NOTE
Identities and circumstances of individuals discussed in this book have been changed to protect confidentiality. Any resemblance to actual persons, living or dead, is entirely coincidental.

Cover design by Marylouise E. Doyle.

Library of Congress Cataloging-in-Publication Data

Menz, Robert L.
    A pastoral counselor's model for wellness in the workplace : psychergonomics / Robert Menz.
        p. cm.
    Includes bibliographical references and index.
    ISBN 0-7890-1853-5 (hardcover : alk. paper)—ISBN 0-7890-1854-3 (softcover : alk. paper)
    1. Employees—Pastoral counseling of. 2. Chaplains, Industrial. I. Title.

BV2695.W6 M46 2003
253.5'2—dc21

                                      2002013039

This book is dedicated to the
wellness
of our children—grown and cherished
their spouses—known and affirmed
and
for the *blessings* given us in
Hannah, Jeffrey, and Madeline
our first three grandchildren
and indeed
to the *promise* of more
grandblessings

ABOUT THE AUTHOR

Robert L. Menz, DMin, is Employee Counselor for the Copeland Corporation in Sidney, Ohio, Executive Director of the Shelby County Chaplaincy Board in Sidney, and is an adjunct faculty member at Edison State Community College in Piqua, Ohio. Dr. Menz is a Fellow in the American Association of Pastoral Counselors, a Diplomate in the American Psychotherapy Association, Board Certified in the Association of Professional Chaplains, and a Certified Employee Assistance Professional in the Employee Assistance Professionals Association. He is the author of *A Memoir of Pastoral Counseling Practice* (Haworth Press), and his work has appeared in several professional journals.

CONTENTS

Preface

Business and industry have given much attention in the past several years to health in the workplace. Since a bulk of health expenses are absorbed by companies and organizations, accidents, injuries, and illness will continue to be matters of great concern to them. Presently, many companies have protocols in place to minimize these accidents and injuries with safety and ergonomics procedures. However, progressive companies such as the Copeland Corporation, where I serve, are looking beyond ergonomics to include concepts of wellness both in and out of the workplace. Employers can easily calculate the costs of medical expenses such as back strains and sprains, repetitive motion injuries, heart disease, and addictions, but these employers must also consider that they may spend more on emotional stress and its consequences than on cancer in its many forms. Conflict and marital discord may do more to disrupt the health of employees than all cardiovascular diseases combined. When the repercussions of mental illnesses are examined from various perspectives, they involve expenses that go far beyond health care.

My goal in writing this book is to illuminate the holistic interconnectedness of health in the workplace. Perhaps this is evident to me because I work with it. Similar to stereoimage art, if one is intent on seeing what is beyond the surface, it usually doesn't require much effort, and the real image pops out. It is beyond the scope of this work to teach psychotherapy, to reveal all that mental health professionals are involved with, or to provide a how-to manual for the human resources departments. One cannot learn from a book how to treat depression, conflicts, chemical dependency, or the sundry other problems that manifest themselves in the workplace. There are many professional disciplines capable of offering intervention to clarify or treat a problem to which a manager can refer a troubled employee. Psychologists, psychiatrists, employee assistance professionals, and social workers quickly come to mind. However, there is another discipline eminently prepared to accomplish health care interventions:

the ministers trained in health care and psychotherapy who specialize in psychergonomics.

It is my hope and expectation that this introduction to psychergonomics will broaden the base of potential therapeutic interventions. Psychergonomics is defined in Chapter 1 and further discussed in Chapter 3. Briefly, *psychergonomics is an extension of the concept of ergonomics that includes the holistic interconnectedness of mind, body, and spirit that impacts wellness in the workplace.* Further communicating this concept will augment caregiving and reveal the multifaceted dimensions of human health and safety. I proceed with the awareness that if this information helps the professional care provider, it will help the employee; if it helps the employee, it will help the company; and if it helps the company, it will help the employee. We need for this cycle to begin.

Previously, help for troubled employees was most often provided through employee assistance programs (EAPs) which were born out of occupational alcoholism programs that helped employees with alcohol addiction and alcohol abuse issues. As intervention matured into a comprehensive array of assistance, all of the aforementioned professionals have assisted with care. The current holistic model of care that includes the mind, body, *and spirit* would seem to recommend looking to the highly trained specialized ministers for help with a variety of problems. The professional chaplain or pastoral psychotherapist may assist in structuring programs and systems to not only help troubled employees but also to educate employees about sound wellness practices in order to avert potential behaviors that would be holistically detrimental.

Historically, balancing factors have contributed to the success of programs that help employees. In the 1930s and 1940s EAPs emerged primarily to help alcoholics with their drinking problems. Stern confrontation blended with therapeutic intervention to modify behaviors and create a safer work environment. Care and confrontation seems to be the pivot for growth in most of life's difficulties. Howard Clinebell, a renowned pastoral psychotherapist, presents this concept in his book *Contemporary Growth Therapies* (1981). Clinebell offers a formula equating growth to caring and acceptance plus confrontation and reality.

In the past fifty years, programs that assist employees have evolved beyond addressing drinking problems to consider the comprehensive array of difficulties which employers and employees must confront. As we begin this new millennium, these employee assistance programs may continue this trend by incorporating a holistic view of health in the workplace.

About fifteen years ago, while having a complete physical, I was asked by my physician, "Do you wear your seat belt?" I remember thinking, "What does that have to do with my health?" Since then the paradigm has shifted. Most of us now appreciate the relevance of that question to our health. Our awareness of cause and effect in other areas of our health, however, is not that complete.

As the title depicts, this book is directed toward chaplains and pastoral counselors in the workplace. It is my intent to illuminate subtle dynamics in the workplace that can be addressed in order to enhance harmony and health. These dynamics are so universal, however, that I expect this information to be beneficial for all helping professions, particularly in the arenas of mental health and addictions. Medical doctors, social workers, human resource managers, psychologists, and employee assistance professionals will all connect with the concepts and dynamics found within these pages.

The purpose of this book is to shift our paradigm of wellness in the workplace to understand and appreciate a more comprehensive model of health and well-being. We must be aware that a conflict in the employee's family will make a difference in job performance. The old directive, "Leave your personal problems at the door" is easier said than done. If we think that our home life does not affect our work life or vice versa, we must think again. We are interpersonally and intrapersonally connected.

There is now, therefore, a need for confrontation. This confrontation will not occur with a specific individual or even with a given health problem. It is time to confront the old paradigm of illness. Illness and injury do not result from only simple linear causes. A shift from the old conceptual framework should be embraced for reasons that go beyond cost effectiveness and good business sense. Given what we now know about the holistic model of health care, shifting the paradigm is the right thing to do. It is the responsible and caring thing to do. This book will address some of the balancing factors in making such a shift.

PART I:
CHAPLAINS AND PASTORAL COUNSELORS IN THE WORKPLACE

Professional health care chaplains and credentialed pastoral psychotherapists are poised to be an appropriate vehicle and professional means by which psychosocial-spiritual issues in the workplace may be addressed.

Chapter 1

Introduction

No [one] can reveal to you aught but that which already lies half asleep in the dawning of your knowledge.

Kahlil Gibran

. . . an overwhelming number of Americans recognize the close link between spiritual faith, religious values, and mental health, and would prefer to seek assistance from a mental health professional who recognizes and can integrate spiritual values into the course of treatment.

Roy Woodruff

Psychergonomics is a concept and a process toward wholeness that integrates multifarious dimensions of wellness and the human experience. Psychergonomics will be further discussed in this chapter and Part II of this book, especially Chapter 3 which is primarily dedicated to the subject.

First, however, I would like to direct attention to a profession that is eminently qualified to address this subject. Psychergonomics calls for embracing wholeness. When the spiritual dimension is ignored, as it often is, well-being is lacking and wholeness is missed. Many mental health professionals do respect and incorporate spirituality into their practice. These professionals are already prepared to pursue the ideas discussed in this book. Another profession, however, also stands prepared to implement wholeness into their practice, but may be overlooked when it comes to wellness in the workplace. Specifically, I am referring to ministers who are trained and credentialed in health care and psychotherapy. Spirituality has become an increasingly popular theme over the past several years. Particularly since the terrorist attacks of September 11, 2001, the search for fundamental understanding and meaningfulness has been overwhelming.

A 1957 study that was repeated in 1976 brought to light the American propensity to value spirituality. The resulting book, *Mental Health in America,* revealed that the American public more often turned to clergy with their personal problems than to physicians, psychiatrists, psychologists, or any other mental health professional (Veroff, Kulka, and Dorran, 1981). More recent research shows that this trend continues. The American Association of Pastoral Counselors (AAPC) and the Samaritan Institute joined to fund a new expanded survey that was completed in November 2000 by Greenburg Quinlan Research, Inc., of Washington, DC. Dr. Roy Woodruff, executive director of AAPC, reported the research findings in an AAPC publication. Some of the results follow.

- Eighty-three percent of respondents feel their spiritual faith and religious beliefs are closely tied to their state of mental and emotional health.
- Seventy-five percent of respondents say it is important to see a professional counselor who integrates their values and beliefs into the counseling process.
- Sixty-nine percent believe it would be important to seek a professional counselor who represents spiritual values and beliefs if they had a serious problem that required counseling.
- Seventy-seven percent say it would be important for an elderly parent or relative who was in need of treatment to get assistance from a mental health professional who knew and understood the relative's spiritual beliefs and values.
- Perhaps most remarkable, more people prefer pastoral counselors and others with religious training to any other category of professional mental health caregiver.

The researchers at Greenburg Quinlan concluded:

> There appears to be a favorable environment for the type of role pastoral counselors can play, especially for the growing elderly population. Voters say it is important to them that mental health counselors be able to integrate spiritual health and mental health in the course of counseling. These data also show a widely held belief that emotional well being is closely linked with spiritual faith. (Woodruff, 2001, p. 2)

A LOOK AT PROFESSIONAL CHAPLAINS

Since each religion or denomination sets its own standards for whom they will ordain, the requirements for a bonafide clergyperson spans the gamut. Some faith groups do not require any college degree. Most mainstream groups require a master's degree. Beyond churches, many organizations also employ the services of a chaplain. A chaplain is a clergyperson who works in an ecumenical setting, yet not all of these settings require special certification of their chaplains. Within this book, the word chaplain refers to a professional that has specialized training far beyond the college and seminary experience.

In Larry VandeCreek and Laurel Burton's white paper, *Professional Chaplaincy: Its Role and Importance in Health Care,* a succinct overview of chaplains is offered.

Professional chaplains are theologically and clinically trained clergy or lay persons whose work reflects:
- Sensitivity to multi-cultural and multi-faith realities
- Respect for patients' spiritual or religious preferences
- Understanding of the impact of illness on individuals and their caregivers
- Knowledge of health care organizational structure and dynamics
- Accountability as part of a professional patient care team
- Accountability to their faith groups

In North America, chaplains are certified by at least one of the national organizations that sponsor this paper and are recognized by the Joint Commission for Accreditation of Pastoral Services.
- Association for Clinical Pastoral Education (approximately 1,000 members)
- Association of Professional Chaplains (approximately 3,700 members)
- The Canadian Association for Pastoral Practice and Education (approximately 1,000 members)
- National Association of Catholic Chaplains (approximately 4,000 members)
- National Association of Jewish Chaplains (approximately 400 members)

Whether in the United States or Canada, acquiring and maintaining certification as a professional chaplain requires:
- Graduate theological education or its equivalency
- Endorsement by a faith group or a demonstrated connection to a recognized religious community
- Clinical pastoral education equivalent to one year of postgraduate training in an accredited program recognized by the constituent organizations
- Demonstrated clinical competence
- Completing annual continuing education requirements
- Adherence to a code of professional ethics for health care chaplains
- Professional growth in competencies demonstrated in peer review (VandeCreek and Burton, 2001, p. 7)

In 1998, the Association of Professional Chaplains was established when the former College of Chaplains and the Association of Mental Health Clergy merged. The Association of Professional Chaplains certifies and serves chaplains in all types of health and human services settings representing more than 150 faith groups and comprising twenty specialty groups.

Clinical Pastoral Education

Clinical pastoral education (CPE) is a dynamic and experiential training program that is requisite to becoming a professional chaplain. Under professional supervision and peer review, the CPE student learns through personal reflection, pastoral formation, and professional competence as he or she moves toward a given specialty. Components of CPE include didactic presentations, verbatim/case presentations, helping skills lab, interpersonal relations seminar, and theological/psychological integration. A unit of CPE constitutes at least 400 hours of these mentioned activities in addition to clinical practice. A minimum of four units is required to stand before a committee to assess readiness for certification by one of the certifying organizations. Most professional chaplains have completed more than four units, and many have over ten units of CPE. In my CPE experiences at the Veterans Hospital in Kansas City, Missouri, and the Baptist Memorial Hospital in Kansas City, Missouri, there were very few medical procedures and surgeries that I did not have opportunity to observe in a student capacity. Likewise, there were very few medical-psychosocial-spiritual situations that I was not exposed to. Personally speaking, hour for hour and dollar for dollar, CPE has been the most meaningful educational experience of my career.

Psychergonomics calls for a broad exposure to the dynamics of health. Many caring professions provide a holistic understanding of wellness. However, clinically trained, board-certified chaplains are certainly poised to embrace the holistic concept.

A LOOK AT PASTORAL COUNSELORS

Before there were psychotherapists, there were "men of the cloth." Times have changed. A minister today would not think of practicing medicine or law unless he or she had the license to do so. Yet despite the emergence of the relatively new discipline of psychotherapy, clergy are still called upon for counsel. It is not atypical for a seminarian to learn the limits of his or her training, and the art of referral is an important lesson to learn early in ministry. Yet to varying degrees, most clerics offer some form of counseling.

Within this book, however, the term pastoral counselor is not a reference to pastors who counsel but a reference to a specialized discipline for those who have been trained in theology and credentialed in psychotherapy. Or, stated another way, pastoral counselors are certified mental health professionals who have had in-depth religious or theological training.

The intentional integration of religion and psychology for psychotherapeutic purposes began when renowned minister Norman Vincent Peale and psychiatrist Smiley Blanton established the American Foundation of Religion and Psychiatry in the 1930s. This foundation is now the well-known Institute of Religion and Health. In the decades that followed, pastoral counseling continued to mature and find a place in the mental health community.

In 1963, the American Association of Pastoral Counselors (AAPC) was founded. The purpose of AAPC is to certify pastoral counselors, accredit pastoral counseling centers, and approve training programs. AAPC represents a set of professional standards for approximately

3,200 pastoral counselors and 100 pastoral counseling centers in North America and around the world.

In the AAPC publication, *Pastoral Counseling: A National Mental Health Resource,* the AAPC requirements for pastoral counselors are outlined.

> Pastoral Counselors certified by the American Association of Pastoral Counselors are highly educated professionals. By studying theology as well as psychology, Pastoral Counselors are trained in two disciplines instead of one. The typical education and training for the AAPC Pastoral Counselor at the membership level of Fellow consists of a Bachelor's Degree from a college or university, a 3 year professional degree from a seminary, and a specialized masters or doctoral degree in the field [of mental health]. A significant portion of this education is spent in clinical training. The primary levels of AAPC certified membership are: Member—an apprentice certification; Fellow—indicating full clinical competence; Diplomate—which qualifies one to work as a supervisor of ministers and Pastoral Counselors. (AAPC, 2000, p. 2)

An AAPC fellow is required to complete a total of 1,625 hours of supervised experience, including 250 hours of direct supervision in a variety of situations. The typical fellow in AAPC, with two graduate degrees and training in two disciplines, often has more education than his or her counterpart in other mental health specialties.

Pastoral counselors stand in good company with such mental health giants as Carl Jung, William James, Abraham Maslow, Karl Menninger, and M. Scott Peck who all sought to blend the dimensions of psychology and spirituality in the pursuit of human wholeness.

PROGRAM MODELS

Many companies have programs or departments that provide assistance to troubled workers. Companies sometimes vary in what they name their employee assistance programs. Employee counseling, employee services, wellness program, health services, and employee assistance are not uncommon labels placed on these programs offering help to employees. These services may be internal or external to the company's organizational structure, may be provided on site or off site, and may be administered by highly respected professionals or committed co-workers. The following model, which this writer operates within, incorporates the best of the typical internal and external programs. In this model the company engages community leaders representing a broad range of vocations and expertise to serve as a board of directors for the program. The program's structure and procedures are addressed from the outset. Together, the board of directors and key company personnel agree on the fundamental ingredients of the program and its personnel. With this structure it has all the strengths of an internal program (that is, an intimate awareness of the organization and its processes, an on-site office, and high credibility with managers). At the same time, the program is managed by the board of directors, lending itself to the fundamental strengths of an external program (which includes a perception that it is not a part of management and an off-site office which lends itself to better confidentiality). Everyone knows that personal and personnel files will never mix, and issues of confidentiality are accepted.

In any regard, a successful program will identify and assist employees, and usually their family members, in improving and/or correcting problems related to alcohol and drug abuse, marital and family difficulties, stress and other emotional distress, and legal and financial issues. It is my expectation that with the growing awareness of holistic interconnectedness, and henceforth the concept of psychergonomics, these goals will be accomplished in a more comprehensive fashion. Certainly, in a time of quality management and international standards, corporations will expect professionalism par excellence from their employee assistance provider.

DEFINITIONS

Already, within the introductory pages of this book, words have been used that are not found in everyday speech and will be unknown to some readers. Since these words provide the foundation for this book and will be used repeatedly, precise definitions are in order. Some of these words have been partially defined in the context in which they have been introduced. Others need further clarification before we proceed.

Ergonomics

Ergonomics became a common term in the workplace during the 1980s and 1990s. Ergonomics is *an applied science concerned with the study of the problems that people have in adjusting to their environment—especially adapting work conditions to suit the worker. Issues such as lifting, repetitive motions, and arranging the workstation to fit the employee are addressed to prevent or minimize strains, injuries, and surgeries.* Workplace injuries are costly to both employers and employees. Employees do not want to be injured at their jobs, and employers must find ways to reduce the financial harm that results when an employee is hurt and worker compensation claims are made. Consequently, ergonomics considers ways to manipulate the work site, the sequence, and the flow to make the job better fit the employee. Sometimes the employee is given a platform to stand on to make his or her work more posture neutral. Sometimes it is a matter of adjusting the height of the chair, putting a soft mat on a concrete floor, adding power tools, improving lighting, or rotating jobs. All of these interventions are extremely cost effective if they reduce the frequency and severity of injuries. Smart employers are not waiting for outside agencies to point out hazards or safety issues. Instead, they aggressively seek to understand how a specific job can be made safer and ergonomically sound for a given employee.

Psychergonomics

Psychergonomics is, to my knowledge, a new term. I coin this term here to *extend the understanding of ergonomics to include a more holistic model of health and suggest that holistic assistance programs and holistically oriented professionals are the suitable means to accomplish mind-body-spirit wellness in the workplace.* As the paradigm of health care has shifted from disease and illness to health and wellness, the workplace must shift from reactive to proactive intervention. The hurt caused, the damage done, and the money spent to clean up or respond to employee troubles must begin to shift to the front end of the spectrum. Prevention is the key to psychergonomics. The "pay me now or pay me later" concept is paramount. Any monies spent for educating, equipping, and preventing will indeed be cost effective. Hopefully, within the pages to come, an understanding will be achieved, a concept will be accepted, and psychergonomics will be assumed.

Even though the concept of psychergonomics points to a comprehensive view of wellness, I wish to point out an obvious omission. The term does not allude to the many systems of the body such as the nervous, muscular, respiratory, and circulatory systems. It does not imply any concern about biology or genetics. Finally, it does not overtly reveal a concern for the spiritual dimension. However, the word psyche is not only a reference to the mind; in a less familiar sense, the psyche is the seat of the soul. Therefore, my use of this term seeks to consolidate the interconnectedness of our being (mind, body, and spirit) and illustrate how this connectedness is relevant to wellness in the workplace.

There seems to be no grand unified theory that reveals how an argument with one's spouse leads to disease X or injury Y. An infinite number of variables play into the dynamics of life. However, the dynamics of life is the point. Humans are neither static nor unidimensional; we are multifaceted and interconnected. When I recognize this in the context of health in the workplace, I label it "psychergonomics." It is not my task to trace a domino effect or explain the dynamics or interconnectedness of health (in or out of the workplace), but simply to point out that this relationship exists.

A company's well-being is dependent upon many variables, only one of which is the employees. An employee's well-being is likewise dependent upon many variables. *Psychergonomics is the attention given to wellness in the workplace by means of education, prevention, treatment, and therapy.*

PARADIGM SHIFT

Today, with the new social awareness of wellness and the paradigm shift in health care, workplace injuries can no longer be understood in a one-dimensional mode. In the 1970s, work injuries included cuts, bruises, breaks, burns, ruptures, and other physical maladies. Today, with a holistic model of understanding, it may be determined that injuries or accidents were due to depression or substance abuse, and high blood pressure is the result of being "worried sick."

There have been such rapid and drastic changes in health care in the past twenty-five years that this paradigm shift is not immediately appreciated. I remember when a holistic view of health was considered by many to be mystical, mythical, and scientifically unfounded. The adaptation of a holistic view is a new concept only in parts of the Western world that previously moved in a one-track (physical) epistemological point of view. Now, we have not so much found as reclaimed the concept that we are mind, body, and spirit, an idea that has long existed in other cultures. It is not as much that we are a body that has a mind and spirit as it is that we *are* body, we *are* mind, we *are* spirit, and what happens in one dimension of our existence impacts the other dimensions. So, specialized medicine remains, but other treatment arenas, such as family practice, seek to integrate and address the whole patient, indicating a new emphasis on human values and patient wishes. The body is not seen so much as a machine in good or bad repair as it is a dynamic system influenced by family, friends, workplace, and culture. Psychosomatic illness does not mean that one thinks that he or she is sick, but rather how the psyche (mind) is affecting the soma (body) and vice versa.

More has been contributed to the health of the human race from outside the health care system than from within it. This may sound anti-health care, but that is not my intent. I am merely stating a fact. Countless diseases and deaths have been avoided by providing clean drinking water, screens on windows, and seat belts in automobiles. Awareness of environmental hazards has saved limbs and avoided cancers. Being aware of what constitutes a healthy lifestyle and being alert to hazardous situations promotes personal health.

One may think of health intervention on four levels. The first level is *medical intervention.* When the body is broken, get it fixed! This level, of course, is the traditional model for intervention. This level will always be available to us, yet historically our society has too often taken health for granted until it is lost.

Another level is *structural prevention* in which attention is given to changing the society or environment within which people work and live. Examples include speed limits on the roadways, seat belts in automobiles, and smoke detectors in homes. Over the past decade, significant attention has been given to such issues as ergonomic awareness and laws regulating drinking alcohol and driving. Incorporating a healthy mind-set within the very structure of organizations will build a healthy foundation for our children and their children.

The third level, *pro-wellness,* fosters a social climate of well-being. Pro-wellness is primarily conceptual and involves advocating healthy choices and avoiding unhealthy practices such as a company that incorporates wellness practices into all levels of the organization. After all, the best way to stay well is to avoid sickness and injury.

Finally, *behavioral prevention* involves claiming ultimate authority and responsibility over personal wellness. These individuals have become convinced that they alone are ultimately responsible for their well-being. Knowledge is power, and understanding is healthy. Most employers have utilized the first three interventions with degrees of success. Accomplishing behavioral prevention reaps substantial benefits.

Benefits

Even though I have not completed research to empirically validate the cost effectiveness of the employee services program at the Copeland Corporation, where I serve, I can conclude that the savings are substantial for four primary reasons. First, the bulk of the mental health counseling (psychosocial and marriage-family) is confidentially provided by myself. Second, I refer employees to treatment centers or psychologists/psychiatrists who have a proven track record in helping persons with the situation for which they are referred. Third, I have a strong community presence and involvement. This networking necessitates a mutual respect and accountability with colleagues from multifarious disciplines. Finally, I provide consultation and education on a variety of psychosocial-spiritual issues. Educational programs are offered on a structured and informal basis, and consultation is provided in timely fashion on such issues as current trends in mental health, the dynamics of domestic violence, and the expected consequences of a third DUI offense.

Substance abuse, illnesses, and accidents cost companies billions of dollars every month. Exact figures are elusive and limited in what they measure. Historically this problem has too often been looked at in a physical, one-dimensional model. I suggest that just as wellness in health care must look at the total picture, wellness among workers must be considered in a holistic fashion. That is, an alcoholic employee may need care and confrontation and even treatment, yet the enabling behavior of the codependent family member also needs to be addressed. Putting a precise price tag on the costs of substance abuse, family and marital problems, emotional troubles, and financial issues is beyond the focus of this book. No simple or linear cause-and-effect model exists for understanding accidents, injuries, or illnesses that affect persons in the workplace. A more complex model may only be appreciated in the context of *psychergonomics*.

Chapter 2

Relevant Employee Counselor Issues

Some . . . see things as they are and say "why?"
I dream of things that never were and say "why not?"

Robert F. Kennedy

Everything should be made as simple as possible, but not simpler.

Albert Einstein

Mental health professionals proceed from a broad brush perspective. Employee counselors reach out to all employees. Intervention must be available for chemical dependency, marriage and family problems, and the seemingly boundless issues facing the worker and his or her family members in the twenty-first century. The professional needs to possess a working knowledge of the organization he or she is working in as well as maintain expertise in mental health, addictions, and the art of referral. Just as a psychotherapist owns, understands, and uses the DSM-IV, the employee counselor must also be acquainted with the structure and policies of the organization.

As has already been stated, this is not a how-to book on what employee counselors are expected to be knowledgeable about. My intent is to emphasize the importance of utilizing existing knowledge in proactive ways to promote wellness and wholeness in the workforce and workplace. To accomplish this, certain issues must be recognized. The four issues described in this chapter are all relevant to the workplace, but they are not the only relevant issues. A comprehensive summary would be quite lengthy indeed. Nonetheless, it is my hope that illuminating the importance of marketing, confidentiality, workplace violence, and community will serve as an impetus to motivate like concern for the many other issues found within the context of the workplace.

MARKETING AND COMMUNITY RELATIONS

It may be important to the company to validate the cost effectiveness of the employee counselor's program, but what if clients or patients do not utilize the service? If this is the case, the program cannot survive. Therefore, communicating the essence of the service is imperative. This communication, when done intentionally and directionally, is a major part of marketing. What is a sound marketing approach for an employee assistance and counseling program? Well, just as nothing breeds success like success, nothing promotes a good program like having a good program. If you are helping people, word gets around. To me, positive comments by word of mouth are the best form of public relations and positive advertising. The product that an employee counselor sells—psychotherapy, chemical dependency treatment, and referral—is not enough. These professionals must also sell service. In a nutshell, marketing is fulfilling the customer's needs.

What kind of training can be offered and to whom? What can be done at the company health fair? How can technology or e-mail promote the program? Is the response rate for employees and employers adequate? Are utilization reports timely and is the utilization rate above the norm range of 5 to 10 percent? Do reports go to the highest possible level? These and other questions are what the professional counselor must be concerned with.

It is important that all new employees are informed of the program upon their initial orientation. This signifies, among other things, that there is companywide recognition and support of the program from the top down. Benefits such as insurance and vacation are clarified and the counseling benefits are presented at the same time (in my case, in booklet form), providing an invitation to utilize and access these services without stigma. Managers and supervisors are periodically reminded to be attentive to their employees' struggles and make timely and appropriate referrals.

Posters and banners are also a meaningful way to get the word out. I've designed a poster with a Christmas tree in which each ornament is labeled with a life struggle. Another poster depicted a road map in which direction signs point to different problems. Each poster will have an invitation to call me and the statement, "All conversations held in the strictest confidence." These posters are updated periodically, and some poster can always be seen somewhere in the company.

Other literature that is informational or educational is also advertising for the program. This material may be distributed through health fairs, plant or businesswide gatherings, mailings, or paycheck inserts.

Utilization of the local media is another way to get the word out and educate your constituency. Articles in the local newspaper on mental health and healthy lifestyles are a case in point. These articles are read not only by the employees of your company, they are also read by other professionals in your community that help make up the network of helping people and organizations that offer assistance to employees when referrals are made.

This, of course, leads to the importance of establishing and maintaining positive professional ties within the community. I serve on many boards and agencies. When it is time for me to make a referral, I have a better perspective of who or what would be the most beneficial and meaningful referral source given the unique circumstances of the employee seeking help. Conversely, as others in the community learn of the program that I serve, community relations are enhanced as well. This is all accomplished in cyclical fashion.

It is important to be explicit on communicating what your program is and how it can help. The more persistent and consistent one's efforts are, the better exposure the program receives. That is, assuming that what you offer is good and is helpful.

Yet, the familiar phrase, "What you do speaks louder than what you say," is entirely relevant here. "Recognizing that integrity is central in ethical life amounts to seeing that personal, occupational, civic, and social life are not radically divisible or separable. If they were, life would be a kind of schizophrenia; . . ." (Delattre, 1984, p. 12). We need to ask: Is the performance consistent with the message? If not, a breech of ethics has occurred. When what we are doing coincides with what we say we are doing, and when people respond and wholeness is enhanced, then good community relations are in process. "Let your light so shine before men, that they may see your good works . . ." (Matthew 5:16) is accomplished whether one recognizes it or not.

It has been my goal to develop a meaningful program of community relations that would seek to accomplish ways by which the programs and services could best be communicated in the area. Affirming the collegial quality and professional expertise of other caregivers in the community and realizing that wholeness requires wellness (physically, spiritually, and mentally) are integral to my understanding of public relations. It is important to avoid claiming that the program is more than it is or to attempt to generate more business than the program can appropriately handle. To do so would not be ethical.

Community relations is not an event—it is a process. Just as one never finishes the task of balancing a moving bicycle, one never completes the task of community relations. Certainly continued refinement and innovation are indicated and appropriate as time progresses.

Whenever the counselor relates to others in the community, the program is engaging in community relations. When counseling is offered, community relations occur. When there is interfacing with the employees and agencies of the community, community relations occur. In that sense, the professional competence and ethical conduct of all persons associated with the program impact upon its community relations. As has already been stated, community relations is a process. The process does not begin when one starts paying attention to it, and the process will not end if one stops all community relations concerns. To stay cognizant of this process is good marketing practice.

CONFIDENTIALITY

Confidentiality is one of the most important features of a successful program. In fact, a program cannot exist unless the clientele has the trust that others will not know of the situation for which he or she is seeking help. A good program will fail if this trust is lost. I once heard a secret defined as "that information shared to only one person at a time." To maintain privileged information in a professional capacity is beyond keeping a secret. It is not being clandestine or stealthy. Confidentiality refers to being responsible and ethical.

Issues of privacy, confidentiality, and privilege, as well as mandatory or discretionary reporting, are distinct yet interrelated. Professional guidelines and state laws offer unique variations, yet substantial common ground exists. For our purposes, confidentiality will generally be regarded as the client's right to have his or her private information obtained, maintained, and guarded from any third party except when consent is granted by the client. Confidentiality is also understood to be the ethical and legal duty of a therapist to not disclose such information without a release authorizing such disclosure or as dictated or permitted by law. Credentialing bodies and licensure boards provide codes of professional conduct that clearly require their professionals not to disclose confidential client information without the client's consent, except as required or allowed by law.

My advertisements refer to the counseling service as being "strictly confidential." This caption alludes to the strictness of protocol. That is, there are professional guidelines, policies, procedures, and legal statutes to follow. I refrain from implying *total* or *absolute* confidentiality. In fact, these do not exist. Depending on the discipline one is operating from and the state one is operating within, applicable ethics and risk factors may supercede confidentiality. For instance, the professional may have a duty to warn or notify authorities if his or her client is homicidal or suicidal. Also, contagious diseases or irresponsibility that would harm others may constitute a duty to warn. Becoming aware of abuse or neglect of children, the elderly, or handicapped persons may necessitate breaking confidentiality. A situation very common to employee counselors occurs when an employee is referred for substance abuse and the employer needs to know that the employee is addressing his or her needs in therapy and overcoming the problem.

In situations where a manager has referred an employee, it is necessary to obtain a release of information from the employee so that the therapist can make the necessary communication with the manager. This consent for disclosure also gives the client the assurance that only information relevant to the concerns will be disclosed. In addition, this information will be shared only with those professionals relevant to the concern. Dilemmas of confidentiality between the client's right to privacy and the employer's right to protect personal safety and property are usually resolved with a completed release of information form. This consent form must include the date, precisely what is to be disclosed, to whom, and for what reason. The client also must be informed of the length of time that the disclosure is valid, his or her right to inspect and copy the record, and the right to revoke the disclosure at any time.

Sometimes the client will ask, "Will this information go any further?" or "What I'm getting ready to say will be confidential, right?"

Many times my answer is, "Sure, as long as it is legal and ethical for me to do so." In some situations, when the client is planning to hurt himself or herself, or someone else, the professional must do everything possible to prevent the harm. Clearly, most questions about confidentiality emphasize the importance that the client's information not be shared with others. However, stating up front that there are circumstances which sometimes supercede confidentiality is important.

Having a consistent and professional policy regarding confidentiality and being able to articulate these responsibilities offers the clients a sense of legal and ethical respect for the program. Yes, there are times in one's professional career that one's legal and ethical responsibility causes him or her to report molestation to the Department of Children Services. There may be times that one must seek legal advice or obtain a court order permitting disclosure to warn an intended victim. This notwithstanding, apart from a signed release of information form, the employee counselor will do well to guard all client information from third parties. In the workplace, the counselor must assume that every employee is a potential client and once a client, always a client.

This does not mean that general dynamics and camouflaged information cannot be presented for educational or supervision purposes, but the information must be presented in such a way as to not reveal the identity of the person presented in the case. Many therapists present cases at professional meetings or in books and journals, yet extreme care must be used to avoid any identifying data.

The time to address the matter of confidentiality is when developing the policies and procedures of an internal program and incorporating them into the program's structure. This concern can also be satisfied in the development of a contract if the program is external. For a more thorough coverage of confidentiality as it applies to employee counseling, a good reference is *Employee Assistance Law Desk Book* (Nye, 1998).

VIOLENCE IN THE WORKPLACE

When I lived in Illinois a number of years ago, I had a physician friend who was the quintessence of the popular doctor of movie fame—Patch Adams. Another friend who had a painful and injured right knee went to my physician friend for treatment. The doctor asked his patient to raise his left pant leg.

"Oh my," the doctor said to his nurse and then ordered, "please take notes. Schedule the operating room for the earliest time for an amputation of the left leg."

"Wait, Doctor," said my friend. "It is my right leg that hurts."

"Oh," the doctor said as he turned again to his nurse. "Please cancel that order. Now raise your right pant leg."

"Oh, yes," the doctor said as he began his touchy examination. "Oh, yes. OK. Hmmm. That's it."

"What is it, Doctor?" replied my friend.

"Your right leg hurts," was the response. "It hurts—that's the problem."

From that point on, rapport was established and the real examination began. Hopefully no one would simply accept, "It hurts," as the final statement for an injured knee.

My point now is this: Why do we accept equally shallow explanations for violence in our society? We already know violence is bad. "He is threatening." "She is controlling." It's almost like saying, "Oh, Judge, that's just the way Charles Manson is." Until we start looking more closely at the fundamental expression of violence saturating our society and the subtle statements of superiority and control found among us, we are not going to get to the root of this problem. Until we understand and accept that emotional abuse and control *is* abuse, we cannot go to the next underlying layer. What I suggest is that there are linkages to violence that connect to issues and human dynamics, that if discussed and understood, could lead to different and less violent behavior.

For instance, we are more often told what we should not do more than we are told what we should do. If one's statements are more akin to the judgmental rhetoric of a Neo-Nazi than expressions of acceptance, seeds of violence may be planted. If prejudicial comments are made, such as, "All women are just alike," "It must be PMS," "I don't understand men at all," "Too much testosterone," then seeds of an abusive nature are sown. Violence begins with expressions of inequality and gestures of control.

Psychological studies are beginning to reveal a correlation between violence in television, the movies, and music and an increase in the violence of the observer and/or hearer (Tischler, 2002). Even television networks that describe themselves as family channels are not immune to this trend.

The media reports the values in America and, at the same time, shapes our values. In this regard, the media participates in the cause and effect. By the time most people reach age eighteen, they will have spent more waking time watching television than doing anything else (U.S. Census Bureau, 1996). Henry Tischler, a leading sociologist, reports that up to one-half of the violence in our society comes from long-term exposure to violent entertainment (Tischler, 2002). The question asked two decades ago, "Who shot J.R.?" may have been made more poignant by asking, "How did you feel about J.R. being shot?" Similar cases may be developed considering the metacommunication impact of print media in its various forms (newspapers, magazines, books), the movie industry, and the music industry. It would be difficult to find an American who has not witnessed a violent scene, whether real or televised.

Violence has been far more intrinsic to our past than we might think. Patriots, humanitarians, nationalists, pioneers, landholders, farmers, and laborers have all used violence as a means to a higher end. Some even consider the Declaration of Independence as a model for legitimizing violence in that it emphasizes people's natural right to overthrow any government that denies basic human rights. Some in our society witness gang wars, cross burning, domestic violence, murders, racism, and an array of other "isms." We have celebrated social bandits such as Jesse James, Billy the Kid, and the Daltons. The Hatfields and McCoys seem to be a perpetual American experience. Presidents are shot and sometimes killed—even the pope isn't safe.

Until recently, however, the workplace was free from the bizarre acts of violence that have now become too common on the evening news. Twenty years ago, such extreme reports of workplace violence were indeed rare. Now, seldom a month goes by without scary outbursts at work somewhere, sometimes as close as down the street. The ice of this social norm has been broken. There are more guns and an undercurrent of acceptance to use them. There are layoffs, downsizing, and an unsettling concept of entitlement. There is stress at home, stress at work, and stress at work that was brought from home. Once associated with dark alleys, gross violence now occurs in well-lit restaurants and sunlit schoolyards. Once the workplace was considered exempt from being sites for murders and massacres. Now murder is the number one cause of death for women in the workplace and the third leading cause of death for men in the workplace (NIOSH, 1997). This data at face value is misleading because men are three times more likely to be murdered on the job than women are.

Data suggests that the majority of homicides are robbery-related crimes. Workplace settings such as the taxicab industry, liquor stores, protective services, gas stations, and jewelry stores represent the greatest threat for workplace homicides (Davenberg and Braverman, 1999). Most nonfatal workplace assaults occur in service settings such as hospitals, nursing homes, and social service settings. In 1997 the National Institute for Occupational Safety and Health (NIOSH) reported that nonfatal assaults in the workplace resulted in more than 876,000 lost workdays and $16 million in lost wages. The National Safe Workplace Institute estimated that workplace violence cost employers $4.2 billion in 1992 (Kaufer and Mattman, 2001).

When we discuss violence in the workplace, what exactly does that mean? I want to expand the stereotypical definition of violence in the workplace to also include harassment, threat, or physical attack. Just as one does not need to touch another person to violate the policy on sexual harassment, one does not have to touch another to be guilty of violence in the workplace. Harassing gestures are those that create a hostile work environment through unwelcome words, actions, and attitudes. Granted, this portion of the definition does not seem to apply until one closely examines the origin of a violent act. A violent reaction is fueled by a sense of injustice. Passive-aggressive comments and harassing actions are seeds of violence and must not be planted, and certainly must be prevented from growing into a full-blown incident. An organization or company policy must start here in the determent of violence. When violence is understood at this level, one quickly sees that violence crosses lines of gender, race, age, education, or any other category being considered.

Violence in the workplace also encompasses threats. Any expression of intent to cause physical harm cannot be tolerated. The threat may be direct such as, "I'm going to kill you." It may be conditional such as, "If you _____, then I will _____." The threat may be expressed through gestures or body language or it may be offered in a third-person comment such as, "Somebody ought to take him out."

When an employee feels powerless, he or she may be more likely to strike out. Angry and retaliatory statements should not be ignored. Red-flag statements such as, "She's trying to push me too far," and "You haven't heard the last of this," must be taken seriously and addressed.

Then, of course, aggression resulting in a physical assault with or without the use of a weapon is violence. Accepting physical attacks as violence is not hard to understand. Getting to the root causes and intervening before major harm is done takes more effort. Beyond the personal harm that violence inflicts, one must consider how violence impacts worker trust, morale, fear, productivity, absenteeism, and turnover. When these factors are recognized, it is imperative to be proactive and not reactive with violence in the workplace.

On average, workplace homicide in the 1980s was about 750 incidents per year. The U.S. Bureau of Labor Statistics reported slightly over 1,000 workplace homicides per year from 1992 to 1995. This trend, however, made a downward turn in 1996 with slightly over 900 homicides in the workplace. There were less than 900 in 1997, and just over 700 in 1998 (less than the average year in the 1980s). This is similar to an overall decline of violent crime in the United States (Sygnatur and Toscano, 2000).

What seems to be of concern, however, is that even though violent crime seems to be declining, we all know of horrendous acts, indeed massacres, that have occurred in the past decade. Likewise, as homicides in schools are on the decline, we do not forget Littleton, Colorado; Springfield, Oregon; Paducah, Kentucky; and Jonesboro, Arkansas. The violence perpetrated in these places is shocking. The good news of improved statistics is tainted with the bad news that our society is facing vicious acts which seem to be unprecedented. Not only has the ice been broken for such extreme deeds, there are those who seek to accomplish copycat crimes.

Because violent acts can occur in any organization, it behooves us all to be proactive in deterring violence in the workplace. Prevention strategies include such actions as:

- Creating good visibility and lighting within and outside the workplace
- Utilizing preemployment screening to the degree allowed by the laws of your state, including drug testing and background checks
- Offering employee training to heighten awareness and provide safety tips
- Developing and frequently referencing a policy on violence in the workplace

- Developing a threat assessment procedure and a threat management team
- Utilizing the employee assistance program or local professionals to provide intervention and consultation
- Developing and utilizing appropriate safety and security measures
- Maintaining a zero tolerance for violence in the workplace
- Recognizing that troubling situations need to be confronted, not ignored

Particularly important is periodic manager and supervisor training. Should a violent or potentially violent act be brought to the attention of the manager, it must be addressed. Zero tolerance does not mean that someone will necessarily be fired. It does mean that the situation will be addressed and the appropriate actions taken. Intervention of this nature is a balancing act. Each incident is unique and calls for specific professional attention. Therefore, I offer these suggestions for managers:

- Have the necessary players at the meeting *without* overwhelming the employee.
- Strategically position everyone in a neutral space *without* cornering the employee.
- Make eye contact *without* staring down.
- Give the person your time *without* giving up control.
- Listen attentively *without* agreeing with what you do not agree with.
- Ask open-ended questions *without* losing focus of why you are there.
- Ask for specific suggestions *without* making an immediate commitment.
- Ask for more information *without* violating your time frame.
- Understand how the person feels/thinks *without* allowing character assassination.

There are also other activities that managers must avoid when dealing with a volatile situation. Managers should avoid:

- Domineering words, actions, and gestures that follow from becoming aggressive.

- Physical contact, finger pointing, a loud voice that results from ignoring your body language.
- Getting trapped into an argument by becoming defensive.
- Getting trapped in a room due to lack of planning.
- Reasoning with an irrational person by proving them wrong.
- Complex and diagnostic interpretations rather than offering simple summaries.
- Allowing unreasonable behavior to escalate by not disengaging and ending the meeting.

Remember, it is never too late in the process to state or restate the ground rules, purpose, and desired outcome of the meeting. The immediate goal is to diffuse the situation, calm the person, and allow intellectual control to replace irrational feelings and behavior.

Much has been written recently on how to predict whether a person will become violent. From my perspective, attention is better spent on preventative measures than on predictive profiles. I must emphasize that profiles have an inherent two-fold risk. One is that just because a person possesses many of the traits in the profile it does not mean that the person is even capable of violence. The other is the assumption that if a person does not possess any of the characteristics of the profile, that he or she is incapable of violence. Each of these may be false. Having said this, however, there seem to be some characterisitics frequently found among those who have been involved in extreme acts of violence. Generally, the offender is a male loner, age thirty-five to forty-five and exhibits the following:

- History of rejection or interpersonal conflict
- Low self-esteem
- Apathy
- History of making unwelcome sexual comments
- Explosive outbursts
- History of making threats of assault (direct or indirect)
- Fascination with and ownership of weapons
- Mistreatment or abuse of animals
- Violence toward inanimate objects
- Recent termination or layoff
- Sense of being treated unjustly
- Indifference toward safety and health of others
- Decreased social connectedness

- Stress related to family, finances, or health
- Obsession with violence or those who commit violence
- Difficulty accepting criticism
- Problem with authority
- Tendency to hold grudges
- Extreme opinions

A more extensive clinical profile may include the following:

- Individual with history of psychosis (i.e., paranoia, schizophrenia, personality disorders, mood swings, depression, talk of suicide)
- Alcohol and/or drug abuse
- Individual with a history of violence
- Out of control, threatening behavior
- Pathological blamer
- Romantic obsession

But again, remember the precautions. These traits in and of themselves are not conclusive for predicting behavior.

Employee counselors, working in tandem with human resource professionals, stand at a strategic place to make a positive impact on this important issue. We must convince employers to prepare for workplace violence like they prepare for product changes. A fearful workplace is an unhealthy workplace. Indeed, security fosters wellness.

There may be a sense of collective employee security in knowing that there is a company protocol regarding a zero-tolerance approach to threats. Stable and predictable outcomes in an age of change are reassuring. In addition, having the company or organization spell out in its policies what will be accepted and what will not, what is right and what is wrong, adds to the company's moral authority.

COMMUNITY

It is important to create a healthy work setting, but we do not spend all of our time at work. We all live in and are connected to the communities that we are a part of. In fact, our personal wellness is so intermingled with the wellness of our society that community cannot be ignored.

I am convinced that we were made for community. We are made to need each other. If we buy into the lie of rugged individualism and islands unto ourselves, we will implode upon ourselves as the leaders of the ancient Roman Empire did with their selfish gestures of conspicuous consumption. If we, on the other hand, realize and affirm that we as individuals are also connected and need to function as a unit, there will be infinite ways to promote community health and thereby enhance our own personal health.

There are consistent ingredients to community health. Change is constant, but so is compassion, respect, care, and love. We are all teachers and students to one another, healers and patients to one another, and psychotherapists and clients to one another. Arrogance is the illusion that we do not need each other and, I think, the pride which separates us from each other. A community to celebrate is a healthy community, and what builds health in our bodies builds health in our communities.

If we viewed humanity from a detached perspective, it would appear that we have replaced the religious quest to save our souls with the secular quest to preserve our bodies. If we pursue health only from an "outside of ourselves" kind of way, we will miss health and well-being. The new paradigm suggests that we are the main ingredient, and attitude and lifestyle is the key.

Allan Luks, executive director of Big Brothers and Big Sisters of New York City and author of *The Healing Power of Doing Good* (1992), cited a classic ten-year study of over 2,700 people living in Tecumseh, Michigan, which indicated that men who did not engage in volunteer work were two and a half times more likely to die from various causes than their peers who did volunteer work. The interpretation from most researchers is that providing helpful services to others is good for health. Connecting with others by giving love, friendship, and gifts is the foundation to true altruism, which is probably the highest expression of optimal health in body, mind, and spirit.

Community comes from the root word *communicare* from which we get the words communication, commune, commute, communism, commons, even communion. So if we are to have community, we must have communion, and to have communion, we must commune. To commune, we must communicate. Communication carries with it gestures of responsible commitment. If community is to be healthy, communication is imperative. It is not that all must agree with the loudest voice, but that all voices must be heard.

M. Scott Peck says that a true community is a safe place where no one is attempting to heal you, convert you, or change you. You are free to be you and to seek your own psychological and spiritual health (1987). According to the transactional analysis model, the ego state where communication occurs is the adult-to-adult state (Harris, 1973). The others are superior or underdog positions where one is guarding the psyche from being overtaken. Only in the adult-to-adult state can we put our guard down and communicate.

Peck also says that, "In and through community lies the salvation of the world" (Peck, 1973, p. 17). At first this statement may seem grandiose, yet with analysis, it rings true from almost every perspective. Together we can do what we cannot do alone. One needs only to read the paper to see the horrendous crimes that can occur when people remove themselves from society where boundaries are identified, health is pursued, and compassion is offered. To act in an isolated and disconnected way causes a social cancer in a community. In fact, that is what cancer is—individual and immature cells doing their own thing and multiplying in disharmony with the collective goal. In addition, almost all disease and illness increases with isolation and weakened social connectedness. The need for relationship and compassion has been so programmed into our being that without it our existence becomes impaired.

This reminds me of a situation that I shared in a previous book:

> Several years ago when in Washington, DC, I was working with a woman in my counseling practice who was requesting something from her husband that wasn't readily forthcoming. I asked her to loan me a 50-cent piece.
>
> "I don't have a 50-cent piece with me."
> "But I would like to illustrate a point."
> "I know, but I don't have 50 cents."
> "It is very important, and I promise I will give it back."
> "I don't have it!"
> "OK," I said.
>
> It is impossible to give something that you do not have. This is true if we are thinking of material items or intangible things like emotional exchanges.

The reverse of this is also true. That is, what one gives is an indication of what one has, or else, how could it be given? One has to be acquainted with love and affection and, indeed, possess some in order to give it. Likewise, to give hostility is to have it to give. What we give is what we have, and what we have is what we give. . . . [G]enerally speaking, one's spirit is lifted by lifting another's spirit. Consequently giving to others is paramount to giving to ourselves. (Menz, 1997, pp. 20-21)

What is a community? We apply the word to almost any collection of persons from a town to a church to a retirement center to our work. Peck says that this is a false use of the word. However, since it is used in those ways, I recommend that it is a shallow use of the word. What differentiates a shallow community from one that promotes health is the presence of communication—of giving and receiving, of accepting and affirming. In this regard, a community must be inclusive. In fact, one of the greatest enemies to community is exclusivity. Groups who exclude others because of their gender, race, life history, political beliefs, and philosophical perspective are groups whose presence leaves something to be desired—namely, a community celebrating wholeness and wellness. True communities are always reaching to extend themselves. A group where everyone agrees is not a community; it is a collection of false personas and people who do not care enough to disagree. A healthy community welcomes tears as well as laughter, fear as well as faith, anger as well as forgiveness, liberals as well as conservatives—for such are you and I. Exclusivity, the great enemy to community, can appear in two forms: excluding others because they are different and fear prevails, and excluding oneself because others are different and self-righteousness prevails.

Nothing brings a community together like intensity—intense circumstance or intense feelings. Intensity breeds intimacy, intimacy breeds vulnerability, and vulnerability breeds communion. I will never forget the community I experienced while on Pr' Line Mountain in the Central Highlands of Vietnam. I disagreed with some of my buddies and they with me, yet we cared for one another in spite of our differences. I worried about my friend Mike Brogan when he left the relative security of the mountain, and he worried and prayed for me when I left. The intensity of sharing our differences and caring created a communion and community among us that transcended time (1970) and space (Southeast Asia) to ensure camaraderie to this very day.

Within the past decade we may ask the people in southern Florida if the crisis of Hurricane Andrew was made better when they experienced community as strangers helped strangers. Ask the people in San Francisco after the earthquake of 1989 if they experienced community as the crisis revealed the sacrifice of people helping people. Ask the people from my home state of Missouri during the floods if they experienced community in the midst of crisis as giving and receiving occurred. Or ask the people of New York City—America's city—was it the crisis that created community? No, it was the helping hand in the midst of the crisis. I think that the twelve-step programs that help millions of people every day are so successful because of the shared crisis in the midst of the fellowship.

One of the marvelous innovations we have witnessed in the past few years is the use of computers to link us to one another and the world. We are on the threshold of experiencing a virtual reality wherein through specially designed gloves and miniature video screens mounted in goggles we will be able to appear in one another's worlds and even "touch" each other. It will give an all new meaning to "reach out and touch someone." We may even see a wedding in the near future where each partner says, "I do" from opposite coasts, and they really have the experience of kissing each other in virtual reality, all of course in "real time." We must realize in this, the so-called information age, that electronic communication is at its best only as an extension of ourselves. We in the United States use computers and electronic media more than any other nation, yet this alone will not create healthier communities.

If it is in our hearts to care for our neighbors, if it is in our intentions to build stronger community, then computers will help us. If we, on the other hand, are waiting for the computer to provide for us a heightened conscience or healthier environment, our wait will be long indeed. There are fearful signs that our interpersonal communication practices in the midst of technological communication have even regressed. Computers are our tools, *not* the other way around. The human spirit is the giver of care, and the community is the forum where caring gestures are extended. When this is accomplished, communication occurs and community is improved.

Another way to affirm health in our community is to recognize that we are one. Everything is connected to and influences everything else. Let me explain. Our bodies have many systems, such as the nervous system, the digestive system, and the cardiovascular system. If a foot gets cut off, the doctor would not say, "Oh, it's OK because your cardiovascular system is fine on the upper part of your body." Our bodies have many systems, but our body is one. Our family is one. Families make larger systems: communities. Communities have many systems such as transportation, sewage and water, and government. Local communities also combine until, at some point, we have a global community. We are one. How the Asian stock market affected the U.S. market in the late 1990s is an example of the global community being one. Systems continue out to the solar system and beyond.

Quantum physicists tell us that we are all a part of this whole, and on a quantum level one entity cannot be distinguished from another. We see a wall, and from our level of perception the wall would stop us, but a neutrino would pass through like a baseball going through our solar system without a concern of collision with another object. Our perception is not on that scale, and so it is hard to appreciate— but that scale does exist.

Here is another example that reveals our connectedness. We know that we cannot create or destroy matter, only change it or transform it. How many of you appreciate the smell of freshly brewed coffee? You know that you do not have invisible tentacles reaching out and touching the coffee. It is rather that the particles of the coffee are saturating the air, the air is bombarding our olfactory system, and the information registers. One may literally ingest coffee without a single sip. Perhaps you have not thought about it, but in a similar fashion, we literally "share" one another.

Each of us, up to this point, has been breathing. Regardless of what else we've been doing, we've been breathing. With your every breath you are taking in about 10^{22} atoms of oxygen and other things and exhaling an equal amount of atoms. You have exchanged that many atoms with every breath, but so has your neighbor, and so have I. Much of what you exhaled was a part of you a brief time earlier, and what you just inhaled will be assimilated in you in the immediate future. Just one year ago, 98 percent of the atoms in our bodies were not there. Now think about it. You and I have become connected and attached or related to our neighbors in a whole new light if we just recognize it. We have been sharing each other and becoming each other in a profound yet real sense, much like those who place cut fingers together and call themselves blood brothers, signifying the blood they exchanged. On the atomic level, we are related. We have a shared experience, but we have also shared much more. Deepak Chopra states in his book *Unconditional Life* (1991) that when we breathe in, we take in millions of atoms that were once a part of and breathed out by Abraham, Christ, and all the saints of the ages. We are much more connected than we recognize. We *are* one. Community is like a living, breathing organism in which the brain, heart, and other organs are interdependent.

We are a part of our community and our community is a part of us. To enhance one is to enhance the other. To ignore one is to ignore the other. To accomplish holistic wellness, we cannot ignore either. To be whole is to recognize that we are one.

PART II:
PSYCHERGONOMICS

The money spent and the attention given to wellness in the workplace can best be understood as a sound investment.

Chapter 3

Psychergonomic Awareness

Your past forms you, whether you like it or not. Each encounter and experience has its own effects, and you're shaped the way the wind shapes a mesquite tree on a plain.

Lance Armstrong
It's Not About the Bike:
My Journey Back to Life

If people are falling over the edge of a cliff and sustaining injuries, the problem could be dealt with by stationing ambulances at the bottom, or erecting a fence at the top. Unfortunately, we put far too much effort into the positioning of ambulances and far too little into the simple approach of erecting fences.

Denis Burkitt

Psychergonomics—the utilization of wellness education, the pursuit of underlying causes of illness, and the proaction of preventative health care as a means of addressing the holistic interconnectedness of mind, body, and spirit which impact wellness and the indirect costs of health care in the workplace.

A number of factors can affect health. Certainly genetics predispose some people to certain diseases. As scientists learn more about the genes responsible for specific illnesses, a person can utilize this information to be more proactive with conscious choices. Such hereditary concerns as the prevalence of cancer, heart disease, alcoholism, or mental illness may be significantly minimized by a proper diet, healthy exercise, lifestyles, and choosing not to drink alcohol.

Other factors such as sex, race, ethnicity, income, education, violent crime, environmental agents, and access to health care can also influence health. Without question, poor health and deadly diseases can befall those who are intent on healthy living. Yet, I submit, an awareness of and a pursuit toward a healthy lifestyle is a worthy goal. Understanding that there may be a connection between financial stress and the failure to track spending, or cholesterol level and diet, or a relationship between an illness and an emotional struggle is meaningful information. The variables involved in personal health are many indeed, yet being willing to consider the psychosocial-spiritual dynamics that affect health are of paramount concern because these factors involve the choices that one makes and consequently the outcome of one's health.

LEADING CAUSES OF DEATH

According to *Health and Wellness: Illness Among Americans,* heart disease is the leading cause of death in the United States, cancer (malignant neoplasm) is second, and cerebrovascular disease ranks third. Other causes of death vary greatly, depending on what sex or race is being considered. Overall, however, the remaining top ten causes of death in the United States in 1999 were: chronic lower respiratory disease, unintentional injuries, diabetes mellitus, pneumonia and influenza, Alzheimer's disease, nephritis, and septicemia. The leading cause of death for all people under forty-five years of age in 2000 was accidents (Wexler, 2003).

A limited number of health-related behaviors contribute significantly to the leading causes of illness and death. Cigarette smoking is a major cause of illness for both men and women. Smokers have twice the risk for heart attack compared to nonsmokers. A recent press release from the World Health Organization (WHO) states that if current trends continue, by the year 2030 tobacco will kill 10 million people a year throughout the world. Half of these deaths will occur during the productive middle years—involving an average loss of twenty to twenty-five years of life (Prentice, 1999).

Another contributor to the leading causes of illness and death is lack of exercise. According to Rose Stamler, in an article published by the Centers for Disease Control and Prevention (CDC), people who are sedentary have twice the risk of heart disease as those who are physically active. Physical activity also reduces the risk of other diseases such as high blood pressure, diabetes, and colon cancer (Stamler, 1999).

When the previous factors, which are in many ways matters of choice, are combined with unhealthy eating habits, we begin to appreciate the ways in which one participates (or fails to participate) in wellness. Considering that diet plays such an important role in such problems as obesity, high blood pressure, high cholesterol, and other chronic diseases and conditions such as diabetes, we must wonder why greater emphasis is not placed on healthy diets. After all, how many people know that eating five servings of fruits and vegetables per day is recommended?

COST OF HEALTH CARE

The United States spent just over 7 percent of its gross domestic product (GDP) on health care in 1970. This can be compared to 13.6 percent of the GDP in 1996. The annual percent increase for health care nearly doubled compared to the average prices paid by consumers for other commodities during the late 1980s and early 1990s. By 1996-1997 the rate of increase for health care was near the consumer price index (Levit, 1997). This, however, may be a brief hiatus as health care costs seem to be on the rise as we proceed into the twenty-first century.

Compared to other countries of similar economic development, the United States spends a larger proportion of its GDP on health care. Other nations that spent large percentages of GDP on health care in 1996 include Germany, Switzerland, France, and Canada. The United States also led other counties in per capita health care spending in 1996, with per capita expenditures of $3,708 (Anderson, 1997).

An obvious question presents itself here. Who has been paying for these health care expenses? In 1997, just over 70 percent of U.S. citizens were covered during part or all of the year by private insurance, mostly through their employers. Most others were covered by government health insurance programs such as Medicare, Medicaid, CHAMPUS (Civilian Health and Medical Plan for the Uniformed Services), and CHAMPVA (Civilian Health and Medical Program of the Department of Veteran's Affairs). Approximately 16 percent of the people in the United States had no insurance during 1997 (Bennefield, 1998). With the major increase in services and expenses of health care in the United States over the past three decades, and with the traditional expectation that employers provide a bulk of insurance coverage, there is a growing awareness that further changes are on the horizon.

One of the changes that has been occurring for at least the past decade is the shifting of a greater part of health care expenses to the employee. We can expect this shifting of burden to continue. Yet, most would accept that there is a point at which both the employer and employee can no longer absorb these escalating costs.

This issue is complicated even more with the positive trend toward increased longevity. In 2000 the average life expectancy at birth was estimated to be 76.9 years. Females, on the average, were expected to live 79.5 years compared to 74.1 years for males. White females were expected to live longer than black females, and white males on the average were expected to live longer than black males. Among black and Hispanic males in 2000, the number of deaths due to homicide, AIDS, and heart disease was much higher than for the overall population (Wexler, 2003).

What needs to be accomplished is the stabilization of health care costs through a systemic understanding of health and wellness. There must be a continued paradigm shift of health and wellness itself. We are behind the eight ball when we continue to focus on disease and seek to regain health. We are pro-wellness when we address the lifestyle choices and unmanaged emotions that subtly and gradually compromise the healing forces within one's being and resolve to abandon a lifestyle that causes sickness.

Medical doctors and other professionals who provide health care are progressively seeking holistic wellness. For the past two decades, at least, a holistic understanding of health has been recognized by some and assimilated by others. Yet, *since our companies and businesses assume significant costs associated with health care, what better place to teach and practice wellness than the workplace itself.*

WELLNESS AND THE CORPORATE SETTING

For employers to assume a degree of responsibility toward wellness makes sense on many fronts. What employer does not know that a happy and healthy worker makes a better worker? Since much of a person's life is spent in the workplace and a respectable amount of the ongoing education of an employee occurs at work, it is reasonable to accept the workplace as a meaningful setting to promote wellness. Indeed, many of the social cues acquired in society, such as responsibility, respect, protocol, and boundaries, are reinforced in the workplace. I submit that outside the family, there may be no other single institution prepared to influence the masses in such an all-encompassing way as the workplace. Any change toward the direction of wellness would render positive results including an impact on a company's bottom line.

Corporate America is structured to effectively calculate the direct costs of employee health. Data including medical costs, worker compensation, absenteeism, disability, and restructuring personnel are readily available. The indirect costs of dysfunctional teamwork, increased safety issues, and lost productivity due to ill health, however, remains largely elusive. There are, though, innovative programs that seek to uncover many of these hidden costs. Wayne Burton, MD, senior vice president and corporate medical director of Bank One in Chicago, and Daniel Conti, PhD, director of Bank One's employee assistance program developed a Worker Productivity Index (WPI). This instrument measures what they call "presenteeism," which is the productivity loss that occurs when workers are on the job but not fully functioning. Burton and Conti applied the index to more than 500 customer service workers to measure how health status affects output. Their findings revealed an interesting correlation: the fewer the health risks, the higher the productivity. Their research measured such health issues as digestive disease, mental health disorders, respiratory disease, injury, musculoskeletal conditions, and cancer. When these issues were factored with health risk variables such as smoking, physical activity, exposure to violence, diabetes, high blood pressure, and high cholesterol, the study was very revealing. Diabetes was by far the most debilitating health risk. The employees lost an average of 4.43 hours per week, most of it attributed to lost productivity, or presenteeism. Their findings led to this conclusion:

> While it's crucial for employee health programs to target the sickest workers and the groups with the highest direct and indirect costs, it's equally important to help the majority of employees at low risk to stay that way. Despite the criticism that on-site

gyms, healthy cafeteria food and the like attract only those who would work out and eat well anyway, supporting the healthy is a vital—and considerably more profitable—way to keep health spending down and productivity up. (Burton and Conti, 1999, pp. 34-36)

Moreover, when companies measure medical and disability costs on a disease-by-disease basis, enlightening data may surface. Paul Greenberg and associates from Analysis Group/Economics in Cambridge, Massachusetts, studied claims from a large Fortune 100 firm which was a self-insured manufacturer. Information on the ten most costly medical conditions were obtained. These included ischemic heart disease, mental illness, cancer, back strain, chest pain, substance abuse, musculoskeletal disease, heart attack, cerebrovascular disease, and non-back strains. Even though two of the top three, ischemic heart disease and cancer, are both associated with long periods of work loss, each is far more likely to accrue high medical costs than to drive up disability spending. For mental health and back strains, the opposite is true. For these two conditions, short-term disability is greater than the medical costs.

When Greenberg took the top ten medical conditions and factored in the disability burden and considered the additional (indirect) costs such as administrative and training expenses to replace workers, and by using an industry standard that utilizes an additional $1.50 in workplace disruption for every $1 of disability charges paid out, a new sequence of the medical conditions emerged. Now mental illness moved to the top of the list and ischemic heart disease (which was at the top of the list when charting the direct costs) moved to the bottom of the list of the total disability burden. This information, if left alone, may not change the bottom line of medical costs. However, this information does reveal the importance of analyzing costs from a variety of perspectives. Seeking to identify such variables as frequency of a claim, the rate of disability for a claim, and the average length of absence for a given condition may provide information helpful in implementing specific disease-management strategies. For instance, musculoskeletal disease is a pervasive condition in the workplace, yet only a small percentage of sufferers file for short-term disability. For this type of illness, perhaps a strategy of education and preventative practices for the entire workforce would be indicated. By contrast, cancer and cerebrovascular disease result in long-term absences but occur much less frequently. Here, specific intervention focusing on the individual patient may be indicated (Greenberg, 1999).

Mental illness is a very costly concern from a disability perspective. Not only is mental illness a prevalent condition in our society, psychosocial-spiritual stressors tend to manifest themselves physically. As the social stigma for mental illness is overcome, and as appropriate and consistent treatment is made available, this will result in a dramatic reduction of direct and indirect medical costs across the board.

TOWARD PSYCHERGONOMICS

When I refer to ergonomics in the workplace, I am addressing the concerns of designing and arranging the work site to further ensure safety and minimize injury. Injuries and accidents are costly concerns economically and emotionally. These work-related occurrences, which end up as claims, are costly workers' compensation expenses. The first known laws regulating workers' compensation are believed to date to the Code of Hammurabi, written in 1800 B.C. (Power and Fung, 1994). At that time Babylon had few slaves in comparison to surrounding civilizations. Codes regulated such concerns as condition of services, work schedules, food, shelter, and wages. The possibility of accidents and liability was also addressed.

Risking life or health in the workplace has never been considered acceptable. In 1970, Congress passed the Occupational Safety and Health Act to ensure U.S. workers the right to safe and healthful work conditions. This notwithstanding, and in spite of improved procedures and practices, workplace hazards continue to inflict a significant toll in both human and economic costs.

Data from the National Institute for Occupational Safety and Health (NIOSH) in 1996 revealed that there were 5.8 million work injuries and 439,000 cases of occupational illness. An average of sixteen U.S. workers die each day from injuries on the job. Furthermore, an estimated 137 additional workers die each day from workplace diseases. Apart from occupational diseases, injuries and deaths in the workplace cost an estimated $121 billion in wages, lost productivity, administrative expenses, and health costs in 1996 alone (NIOSH, 1996).

Currently, innumerable laws govern compensation. Today, companies can quickly provide hard data revealing how much was spent on workers' compensation claims. However, there are many ambiguous expenses that are not as visible. Issues such as absenteeism, productivity, quality of the product, and morale are concerns that impact any company's bottom line. Even concerns of stress being work related are a sign of the times. Prudent companies are ever vigilant of the subtle and invisible dynamics (and expenses) in progress. Such simple modifications as adjustments to the workstation, softer standing pads, correct posture, hoists, and protective gear have done wonders in minimizing injuries and accidents. Certainly the concept of ergonomics has become a common concern in the workplace in the past several years.

Likewise, companies can provide information on how much was spent on the health care of employees and track these expenses over time. There may even be charts and graphs that clarify how many dollars were spent on such things as heart disease (and its various forms), cancer (and its many kinds), and mental health (and the modes of helpful intervention). Research may reveal correlations between heart disease or stroke and high blood pressure. A health care professional may educate employees on the relatedness of high blood pressure and lifestyle (i.e., pointing out the negative effects of distress, smoking, and substance abuse). What impacts the company in terms of health care expenses are not only concerns of quality and productivity but also whether personal circumstances are causing depression. Can grief increase the likelihood of illness? Can drinking on the job increase hostility among coworkers? The answer to these questions, of course, is yes. Nonetheless, measuring how marital conflict influences morale, quality of work, and even safety is a complex task indeed.

Consequently, I would state that psychergonomics is not a strategic formula to initiate a complicated system of cause and effect. It does, rather, point out that this complexity does exist. I'm reminded of a story that I heard years ago: "The boss yelled at his employee, the employee went home and screamed at his wife, the wife spanked her child, the child kicked the dog, the dog chased the cat, and the cat ate the mouse." This sequence may also start at home yet seldom will it avoid contaminating other systems, such as work.

To give attention to the complexities contained in wellness and wholeness, to understand that we are all multidimensional, to appreciate that all of the issues in life play a part in health, lead to the acceptance that these manifold dynamics may provide data that are voluminous. Psychergonomics is not an attempt to identify the original cause of an illness but to accept that there are underlying causes involved when homeostasis is lost.

Most of our emotions can be peeled back to find another (perhaps even more fundamental) emotion underneath. For instance, beneath anger is a threat or a sense of injustice, and even below that is hurt. Underneath and feeding the emotion of jealousy is the feeling of insecurity. Those who blame have a component of shame—and so it goes.

This awareness can certainly be applied to stress. Most everyone complains about stress. To not be stressed is to be atypical. But there is stress in vogue which consists of buzzwords and expected responses and then there is volatile stress which must be addressed. Most people have probably come to realize that it is not busyness that causes stress. Some of the busiest and most productive days have left me energized—not drained. It is when our days unfold in unpredictable and fearful ways that stress becomes overwhelming and unhealthy. Beneath stress is fear and loss of control.

I have chosen the prefix *psyche* not only because of the obvious *psyche*ological implications, but also because of its ancient root meaning, the "seat of the soul." As Carl Jung suggested that the ego is the place where we meet the self, the center of the whole psyche (1963), let us realize that indeed the center of our being is the psyche. What I am suggesting is that the psyche is not only the seat of the soul and the center of our being, the psyche is the core from which life itself flows.

As has already been stated, the unwrapping of wholeness reveals ingredients that are healthy for the employee and beneficial for the employer. A healthy and happy employee may be more productive; consequently, the savings to the company are far more than monies that are not spent on health care. *Psychergonomics is concerned with peeling back the obvious surface causes of an illness, utilizing wellness education, and practicing prevention as the means of addressing the life activities of mind, body, and spirit which impact wellness and the indirect costs of health care in the workplace.*

PREVALENT PSYCHERGONOMIC ISSUES

With the earlier words of this chapter as a preface, I would like to discuss five conditions that produce ill health and complicate good psychosocial-spiritual functioning. These are conditions found in any workplace and are frequently dealt with by employee assistance professionals. First, *mental illness* issues are far greater in our society than many are willing to acknowledge. Second, *depression* creates more suffering than any other malady affecting human kind. Third, *emotional stress* is a condition that most people are acquainted with. Having had a stressful episode, however, does not in and of itself prepare one for the next stressful event. Fourth, *anger* is an emotion that is unavoidable. A person does not choose to become angry. Nonetheless, one may choose what he or she will do with the emotion. Finally, *alcohol abuse* and addiction is a disease that makes the obvious costs (emotional and financial) pale in comparison to the indirect and unseen costs.

I choose these five conditions or illnesses to discuss here for two basic reasons. One, these are topics that I trust every professional counselor has dealt with—at many levels. Second, I expect that the context in which these items are discussed will further illuminate the concept of psychergonomics.

Mental Illness

The need to understand and classify mental disorders has been clear throughout history. Early on, there were two categories to describe mental health: sane and insane. By 1880, seven categories of mental illness were identified (American Psychiatric Association, 2000).

The American Psychiatric Association Committee on Nomenclature and Statistics developed a variant of the *International Classification of Disease*—Sixth Revision (ICD-6), that was published in 1952, and it became the first edition of the *Diagnostic and Statistical Manual: Mental Disorders* (DSM-I). In 1994, the DSM-IV (American

Psychiatric Association) was published and reveals the benefits from substantial research gathered in previous editions.

Even though the title implies a distinction between mental disorders and physical disorders, there remains the dilemma of the mental and emotional manifestations that may be found in physical disorders and the presence of physical symptomology that may be found in mental disorders. This notwithstanding, the DSM-IV offers nearly 400 classifications that may be offered on five axes which seek to facilitate a comprehensive and systematic evaluation.

Mental illnesses are not as easily classified as are physical illnesses. Symptoms may vary in both kind and intensity compared to the symptoms of physical illnesses. In addition, a social stigma continues to be associated with mental illness which keeps some people from seeking treatment. There is also a profound misunderstanding that certain physical symptomology may be aggravated or caused by mental or emotional distress.

According to Manderscheid and Sonnenschein (1994), anxiety disorders (including phobias, panic disorder, and obsessive-compulsive disorder), depression (including bipolar, unipolar major depression, and dysthymia), and substance use disorder (including all alcohol and drug disorders) comprise the three most common mental disorders (over 50 million) in the United States.

In another major study (Regier, 1993), researchers found that approximately 52 million adults in the United States experienced a mental disorder at some time during a year. Even though this represents over 25 percent of the adult population only 28 percent of those affected seek help. Regier reported that every year about 9 million Americans develop mental disorders for the first time, 8 million suffer a relapse, and 35 million are plagued by continuing symptoms. The number of new cases in a year is balanced with an equal number of persons whose disorders go away, leaving the general proportion of persons with mental disorders remaining at a consistent one-fourth of the population. Certainly, when the typical stressors are considered (which are not diagnosed as a mental disorder yet may produce discord or dysfunction), the impact is even greater.

In December 1999, U.S. Surgeon General Dr. David Satcher released *Mental Health: A Report of the Surgeon General.* This report (actually a massive volume) is the first surgeon general's report ever issued on the topic of mental health and mental illness. The report was prepared with the awareness of how mental illnesses contribute to the immense burden of disability. It suggests that mental disorders collectively account for more than 15 percent of the overall incidence of disease (from all causes). Just as health and illness must be seen as points on a continuum, with neither state existing in pure isolation from the other, physical health and mental health (or the lack thereof) must be understood to be inseparable.

The report states that

> [m]ental health and mental illness are not polar opposites but may be thought of as points on a continuum. Mental health is a state of successful performance of mental function, resulting in productive activities, fulfilling relationships with other people, and the ability to adapt to change and to cope with adversity. Mental health is indispensable to personal well-being, family and interpersonal relationships and contributes to community or society. (U.S. Department of Health and Human Services, 1999, p. 4)

Even though well-documented treatments exist for most mental disorders, a negative stigma of public perception and attitude impair accessing appropriate intervention. Other barriers for treatment include a complex and fragmented mental health service system, a perception that effective treatments do not exist, and limited insurance coverage.

Dr. Satcher states in the report's preface that

> [t]hese disparities are viewed readily through the lenses of racial and cultural diversity, age, and gender. A key disparity often hinges on a person's financial status; formidable financial barriers block off needed mental health care from too many people regardless of whether one has health insurance with inadequate mental health benefits, or is one of 44 million Americans who lack insurance. We have allowed stigma and now unwarranted sense of hopelessness about the opportunities for recovery from mental illness to erect these barriers. It is time to take them down. (US DHHS, 1999, p. 4)

In optimistic fashion, the final chapter, "A Vision for the Future," offers an action plan for mental health in the new millennium. This chapter explores the opportunities to overcome these barriers through improved public awareness, improved delivery of state-of-the-art treatments, and reducing financial barriers to treatment.

Certainly these goals can be embraced by employee assistance professionals, and an enhanced understanding of mental health can be achieved in the workplace. Better health, in any dimension, improves the quality of life, the quality of relationships, the collective quality of our communities, and certainly, the quality of our workplace.

Depression

Perhaps the reader has not had a lingering episode that resulted in feelings of total meaninglessness or hopelessness. This is not the case for nearly 11 million people in the United States. Throughout history, professional and artistic people have not been exempt from suffering from depression. Vincent Van Gogh is a case in point. More recent celebrities include the late Charles Schulz, the creator of the comic strip "Peanuts," Mike Wallace, Dick Cavet, and Kathy Cronkite.

I will not discuss any of my current cases here for confidential reasons, but perhaps a couple of stories from early in my practice will capture the pain that is depression.

A hospital call that I was asked to make as a part of my training revealed to me depression in its raw form. I do not remember the elderly person's name, physical condition, or what she looked like. I just remember her agony. During that visit, she said in a whisper, "I'm so thirsty." Knowing that it was permissible to give her fluids, I asked, "May I help you with a glass of water?" After what seemed like a very long time, she said, "No, I would just get thirsty again." This statement was my first exposure to total hopelessness.

Years later I cared for a father whose son had attempted suicide. Early impressions were that the son would die from the shotgun wound which had removed his lower jaw, tongue, teeth, nose, and both eyes. He did not die. Weeks later as I accompanied the father during a hospital visit, I again experienced the intensity of depression. Unable to speak, and with a tracheotomy, the son had learned "yes" and "no" communication with his hands. As I inquired about his restlessness, I was signaled that "yes," he was in great pain. I asked if the pain was from the source of his injury. He indicated, "no," and pointed to his heart. I asked if he was having chest pain, and he pointed to his entire body. With further inquiries, I learned that this intense pain was from his depression—which had led to his suicide attempt. Apparently, no physical pain can rival the melancholic abyss that is the "dark night of the soul."

So what is depression? A psychological reaction to early life experiences? A natural response to a significant loss? A learned behavior style? A biochemical imbalance? A genetic behavioral trait? The answer is all of the above—and probably more.

Most people who are depressed do not kill themselves. However, basically speaking, the people who commit suicide are depressed. Any hints or threats of suicide should be taken seriously. In fact, in 1999 there were more suicides than homicides, making suicide the eleventh leading cause of death in the United States (Wexler, 2003).

Dr. Dale Wright, my first mentor, cautioned me to, "Be careful of the paranoid patients, they can kill you," and "Be careful of the depressed patients, they can kill themselves."

So, how big is this problem of depression? Depression is the most common psychological problem in the United States. Depression is one of the ten most costly illnesses in the United States with an estimated annual total cost of $44 billion (Greenberg et al., 1993). At work, it ranks among the top three problems, following only family crisis and stress (Depression Guideline Panel, 1993). The physical and emotional significance of depression is major, even without factoring in its impact on such things as absenteeism, decreased productivity, and negative effects on family, friends, and co-workers. Depression causes a higher rate of medical visits as physical manifestations of the disease are acknowledged. Furthermore, a chronic illness in and of itself may have a depressive side effect. Many times a physician may overlook the subtle dynamics of depression and treat the obvious or surface problem. Certainly at work depression may go unrecognized and untreated.

Just as group personality is affected by the group's members, so is an organization's character affected by its employees. A group's personality will change as members come and go. An organization's personality is the sum of all its members, and if several are depressed, it impacts the overall climate of the organization. Depression is a whole body illness, encompassing physical, mental, emotional, and spiritual existence. With the prevalence of depression on the increase, we would do well to focus on early detection and appropriate intervention.

There are over twenty diagnostic numbers for various forms of depression in the DSM-IV, but basically they fall in three categories:

1. Depressive reaction—arising from life situations
2. Dysthymia—minor yet chronic (at least two years)
3. Major depression—disabling, interferes with work, sleep, and pleasurable activities (for example, bipolar disorder)

There are many forms of treatment for depression and, again, the intent of this book is not how to do treatment. I will, however, briefly describe the more basic modes of treatment.

One form of treatment is psychotherapy. Psychotherapy has multiple approaches and specific schools of thought (Dayringer, 1995). Behavioral therapists help patients learn how to obtain more satisfaction and rewards through their own actions and how to unlearn the behavioral patterns that contribute to their depression. Behaviorists view depressive reactions as an inappropriate learned pattern in dealing with hostility and guilt. Cognitive therapists help patients change negative styles of thinking and behaving and teach new ways to think more positively. Analysis-oriented therapists view depression as symptomatic of deeper personality disturbances residing in the unconscious. The analytical therapist seeks to resolve the conflicts rooted in childhood.

Another form of treatment, of course, is medication. Three groups of medications have been used in a more traditional and historic sense. They are tricyclics, monoamine oxidase inhibitors, and lithium. There are now two new and very popular classes of antidepressants. The first is fluoxetine, a serotonin reuptake inhibitor, and the other is bupropion, believed to act on the dopaminergic system.

Another form of treatment reserved for the most severe cases is electroconvulsive therapy (ECT). In recent years, ECT has been dramatically improved over its barbaric methods of years past.

Many mind/body practices are helpful with depression. Meditation and relaxation techniques such as deep muscle relaxation are helpful in mild cases. Meditation and prayer activates alpha brain waves and alpha results form a healthy, relaxed experience.

Nutrition and diet are important as well. Foods such as whole grain cereals, lean meats, fruits and vegetables, fish, and low-fat dairy products are healthy. Healthy foods contain the essential vitamins and minerals that facilitate good health. Foods with high sugar content may give a temporary emotional high followed by an emotional crash. Remember, alcohol is a depressant.

Especially during winter months in northern states like my own, people can suffer from seasonal affective disorder (SAD). Exposure to sunlight is therapeutic. (I am not speaking of skin cancer doses.) Full spectrum artificial light is also believed to help.

Finally, laughter is good medicine.

Emotional Stress

An initial reaction may be, "Stress is distressing." After that, it can be quickly acknowledged that this mind-body arousal can save one's life. Stress happens. Stressors are life events, real or imagined, that cause a stress response. Stressors may be physical, emotional, psychological, spiritual, environmental, or economic, but they may not be avoided. How one responds to a stressor is, however, a choice. Failure to learn good habits of stress management will rob people of their health, happiness, and creativity. Mismanaged stress, or distress, fatigue body, mind, and spirit. Properly managed stress, sometimes called eustress, allows people to adapt to the increasing changes of our culture, facilitates personal growth, and aids in the avoidance of harm.

Throughout this book I emphasize the fact that our mind-body-spirit systems are intrinsically woven together. The holistic impact of the physical chemistry generated while experiencing stress will be discussed in a later chapter. I would like to recognize here, however, that thoughts, emotions, and behavior are also interdependent. Whereas feelings are physical sensations, emotions are feelings with names. Anger, sadness, guilt, hope, gratitude, and pride are examples of emotions. In the most basic sense, emotions arouse two fundamental feelings—pain or pleasure. The emotion is either positive (pleasurable) or negative (painful).

Psychiatrist David Viscott (1992) suggests that pain in the present is felt as hurt. Pain of the past is experienced as anger. Pain projected into the future is what we call anxiety. If one fails to express anger, it leads to guilt, and when allowed to drain one's energy, it is called depression. Indeed, much of the harm resulting from stress or distress is due to the mismanagement of emotions.

For the average person, one-third of life activities occur at work. This being the case, significant stressors are experienced at work—as well as opportunities for good management techniques to handle these stressors. An extensive survey designed by the Employee Benefits Division of Northwestern National Life Insurance in 1991 revealed a growing problem of stress in the workplace. The survey addressed data from 1982 to 1990 and revealed that:

• The incidence of stress-related disabilities doubled over this time span.
• Seventy-two percent of American workers experience three or more stress-related conditions very or somewhat often.
• Forty-six percent of American workers feel that their job is very or extremely stressful.
• Ninety-one percent of American workers think that employers must act to reduce stress. (Northwestern National Life, 1991, pp. 5, 9)

Indeed, U.S. workers and their employers consider stress to be reaching harmful levels with the consequences being felt by all involved. Not only is the employee experiencing a growing problem with stress, the employer is faced with greater turnover, lower productivity, higher absenteeism, and higher health care costs.

According to the American Institute of Stress (AIS), stress is the number one health problem. From surveys and research reports over the past two decades, the AIS reports that:

• Job stress is estimated to cost U.S. industry $300 billion annually, as assessed by absenteeism, diminished productivity, employee turnover, direct medical costs, legal and insurance fees, etc.
• 75 to 90 percent of all visits to primary care physicians are for stress-related complaints or disorders.
• Stress has been linked to all the leading causes of death, including heart disease, cancer, lung ailments, accidents, cirrhosis, and suicide.

- An estimated one million workers are absent on an average workday because of stress-related complaints (about one half of the workdays lost annually due to absenteeism).
- The market for stress management programs, products, and services was $9.4 billion in 1995 and about $11 billion in 1999 (AIS, 2000).

Certainly with this kind of data, it is clear that an ounce of prevention may be worth thousands of dollars.

It is impossible for an employer to manage all of the variables that lead to employee stress. The marital, family, financial, legal, and health issues of an employee may be out of the employer's control. However, making available the resources of an employee assistance program may point troubled employees toward the necessary help and resolution of their personal issues. Both a supportive network (external) and coping skills (internal) are necessary to manage stress. The balance between work and home or personal life is also an important factor to consider.

Occupational stressors often include variables that may be addressed in the reduction of stressful situations. Certainly, financial compensation is important to most employees; yet, employees generally prefer to be highly satisfied with most aspects of their work than to be highly compensated. Workers on all levels are seeking the intrinsic rewards that come from enhanced skills and careers. Stressors that come from human interaction, job ambiguity or role conflict, job complexity, bureaucracy, and rapid change may be reduced through an explicit communication system that allows issues to be labeled and corrected before worker frustration becomes intolerable. Other issues such as poor management style, discrimination, ergonomic interests, environmental concerns, and violence in the workplace may result in great havoc if appropriate policies and procedures are lacking in the organization's structure. The more an employer can provide a worker with a sufficient amount of control, adequate leadership, cohesive team involvement, job clarification, and safety, the healthier the workplace will be.

Proactive employers utilize professional employee assistance services to build awareness about job stress and offer classes on stress management which include relaxation techniques, massage, visualization, diet, exercise, the harmful effects of mismanaged stress, and the value of humor.

Anger

Anger is one of the most frequently misunderstood emotions. Anger is regarded as a nasty and dangerous emotion, and in many cases, harmful to one's health. True, anger can be destructive, but this is the result more of mismanaged anger than the basic emotion itself. The anger is not a choice—what one does with anger is. As I said in a previous book:

> . . . To do nothing violates the purpose of the emotion. In essence, anger is present to motivate one to correct an error or to seek to accomplish justice. We have to care, in some way, in order to react to a perceived threat or an unfair situation. We cannot react if we don't care to, and we can't right a wrong if we do nothing.
>
> . . . Our society seems uninformed about and afraid of anger. Anger is one of the seven cardinal sins. Authority figures of the past said, when it comes to anger, "just don't do it." The fear was that if anger went to its limits and turned to rage, people could get hurt. However, it is when anger isn't managed or when it is mismanaged that it turns to rage. Here I would like to add that I'm speaking of the average capacity of a healthy person. We do live in a world with unhealthy psyches that deviate from a healthy norm. But generally, people don't know how to manage their anger because they never *learned* how to managed their anger. Another effect of denying anger is the internalization of the emotion. Not only can one explode with anger, one can implode with depression. One of the causes of depression is anger turned inward. Ironically, not only do severely depressed persons sometimes contemplate (and sometimes accomplish) suicide, depressed people can become unhealthy in a multidimensional sense. In this regard, anger is doing what former authority figures feared. Only here it is not the hurting of the other that needs to be feared; it is the hurting of the self which is being accomplished. (Menz, 1997, pp. 17-19)

The fourth-century B.C. Greek philosopher Aristotle said, "Anyone can be angry—that is easy. But to be angry with the right person, to the right degree, at the right time, for the right purpose, and in the right way—this is not easy." How true. Most of us, when we dare to be honest, have a few embarrassing stories when it comes to anger. Allowing anger to reside in a chronic state can be much more than embarrassing, however; it can be fatal. Living a life filled with anger is like injecting oneself with poison on a regular basis. We know too well that anger can lead to physical and emotional violence. It is far too common to read of road rage, school shootings, and violence in the workplace. The less obvious repercussions of mismanaged anger have even greater consequences. Handling anger poorly can damage relationships, cause problems at work, and create or aggravate health problems. Chronic anger causes the body to pump more adrenaline into the bloodstream (in preparation for "fight or flight"), causes the heart to beat faster, and creates muscle tension and shaky feelings. Failing to deal with anger contributes to heart problems, high blood pressure, headaches, and digestive problems.

In their best-selling book *Anger Kills,* Williams and Williams (1994) cite several studies linking mismanaged anger to ill health, both physically and psychologically. One example involved law students in the 1950s from the University of North Carolina (UNC). The 118 students were given a comprehensive psychological test that measured, among other things, harmful hostility. When these students, now lawyers, were later reviewed, interesting data surfaced. Of the lawyers whose hostility scores had been in the highest quarter of the class, nearly 20 percent were dead by age fifty. Of those whose hostility scores were in the lowest quarter, only 4 percent had died (Williams and Williams, 1994). The book also had examples correlating hostility with unhappiness, negative life events, and less social support.

If mismanaged anger is harmful to the health of the individual, it likewise is damaging the wellness of the organization. The better one understands the emotion of anger, and the quicker one identifies anger within himself or herself, the better prepared one is to appropriately manage anger. To understand that a tense muscle or a sarcastic comment may be signs of unrecognized anger is a start. Internal dialoguing is a necessary step in clarifying the causes of anger. To establish a plan to appropriately express the emotion and let go of that which one is unable to impact is anger management. The philosophy (as voiced in the Serenity Prayer) of changing the things in one's life, or one's world, that can be changed and letting go of that which cannot be changed is a healthy concept.

Some life skills that are important in the management of anger include becoming more assertive, developing better listening skills, having a confidant, and increasing the ability to empathize. Other activities, which will be elaborated on in a later chapter, involving such things as meditation, exercise, laughter, community service, and meaningful hobbies, are beneficial in managing anger. Remember, one of the worst things that one can do with his or her anger is nothing. To do nothing not only prevents one from being redemptive in the world, but it also plants seeds for destruction, which is the ultimate harm that anger can bring.

Alcohol Abuse

It is important to emphasize here that even though alcohol is the drug of choice in the United States, it, of course, is not the only abused substance. Illicit drug use and prescription drug abuse is an alarming obsession, if not addiction, of many. The harm of substance abuse in all of its forms is overwhelming. When tobacco is thrown into the equation, the total costs are shocking indeed. Even though many of the comments made here are applicable to other chemical substances, this section will focus on alcohol abuse. Under certain conditions, alcohol is legal. Indeed in some examples, alcohol may be healthy. This notwithstanding, when considering drug abuse, alcohol represents a significant piece of the pie.

Alcoholism is an illness that is characterized by, among other things, the drinker's consistent inability to choose whether to drink at all or to stop drinking when he or she has consumed too much alcohol. Anyone whose drinking causes problems and who continues to drink is a problem drinker. If there is a dependency on alcohol, or if one cannot control personal behavior, he or she is an alcoholic.

Ethyl alcohol (ethanol), the active ingredient in beer, wine, and hard liquors is the oldest known mood-altering drug. Beer and wine have been used since ancient times in religious rituals, for pain and medicinal purposes, and in communal and individual celebrations. Those who have sought to understand colonial America know that alcohol was a staple commodity and was consumed at the rate of three to seven times the rate of the average U.S. citizen today (Klier, Quiram, and Siegel, 1999).

Klier, Quiram, and Siegel offer a summary of some developmental trends concerning alcohol, including the implementation of the Eighteenth Amendment in 1920 with the Volstead Act which resulted in making the manufacture and sale of alcohol illegal. When organized crime and individual bootleggers were making alcohol readily available to the masses, Prohibition was repealed in 1933 with the Twenty-first Amendment. In 1935, Alcoholics Anonymous was founded in Akron, Ohio, to provide peer support for problem drinkers. With the problem unsolved, Mothers Against Drunk Driving (MADD) was founded in 1980 and has been instrumental in passing 2,300 state laws to deter drunk driving. In 1989 health-warning labels were required on all alcohol beverage containers. The Americans with Disabilities Act classified alcoholism as a disease in 1990. Even though the U.S. Supreme Court refused to identify alcoholism as a disease, it is understood to be a disease by addiction counselors, the medical community, and the insurance industry (Klier, Quiram, and Siegel, 1999).

The National Institute on Alcohol Abuse and Alcoholism (NIAAA, 2001) estimated that the overall cost of alcohol abuse in 1998 was $185 billion. This figure represents criminal justice system costs of alcohol-related crime ($6.3 billion), property and administrative costs of alcohol-related vehicle crashes ($15.7 billion), health care and alcohol treatment expenditures ($26.3 billion), and the estimated $134.2 billion attributed to lost earnings and productivity concerns. Obviously, the problem of alcohol abuse is very significant.

Current estimates indicate that between three and four percent of an average workforce will be deviant drinkers at any one time. This seems to be negligible numbers until the potential impact of any one problem drinker is considered. As stated in an influential book of the 1970s, *Spirits and Demons at Work,*

> [t]he disruptive consequences of deviant drinking may far exceed the cost entailed if four percent of the work force were absent or simply sat at their jobs and did practically nothing. The very essence of a work organization is the interdependence of job performance. Deviance by one employee may "reverberate"

beyond his [or her] workstation or desk, sometimes disrupting an entire organization. (Trice and Roman, 1972, p. 9)

Again, beyond the actual dollar expenses that employers may calculate are costs involving such things as job performance, absenteeism, accidents, morale, employee theft, and interpersonal conflict.

Health problems such as alcohol-induced liver disease are clearly linked to excessive alcohol consumption. According to the NIAAA, approximately 10 to 35 percent of heavy drinkers develop alcoholic hepatitis, and 10 to 20 percent develop cirrhosis. In addition, cirrhosis is the seventh leading cause of death among young and middle-age adults in the United States (NIAAA, 1998).

Given the enormous problems associated with alcohol abuse, there seem to be a couple of positive trends. One is that the U.S. per capita consumption of alcohol has been on the decline since 1980 (Klier, Quiram, and Siegel, 1999). The other concerns the access of treatment. It is estimated that $2 to $10 are saved for every $1 spent on treatment (Hafer, 1998). Certainly it is more costly to ignore the problem than to address it. Ignoring an alcohol problem also has the subtle effect of facilitating the problem. This opens the door to a greater issue of codependency. An organization with codependent tendencies is ill prepared to address alcohol abuse and intervention options. Those organizations that have clear policies and procedures and alert managers and supervisors are poised to help an employee with an alcohol problem.

Informed managers are familiar with defensive and false statements such as: "I cannot be an alcoholic because I do not drink in the morning." "I'm not an alcoholic because I only drink on weekends." "I never fight when I drink, so I can't be an alcoholic." "I'm not an alcoholic, I only drink beer." Denial is powerful and the wise manager must be alert to these expressions of denial.

An employee who is helped to get well is not only a better employee than before; the employee's health contributes to the overall health of the organization.

Regardless of the type of initial intervention and treatment, Alcoholics Anonymous (AA) seems to be a must for ongoing recovery. To stay alcohol free, AA works "the best for the most." Many regard Marty Mann as one of the most influential persons of the twentieth century. Mann, after receiving help in 1939 from the then four-year-old grassroots movement know as AA, began a crusade to educate the whole world about alcoholism. Her impact can not be denied. The famous "Twelve Steps" of AA are now the core of many self-help groups throughout the world. These twelve steps, spiritual in nature, seem to parallel the psychological changes that the problem drinker undergoes as he or she moves toward sobriety. The twelve steps are as follows.

1. We admitted we were powerless over alcohol—that our lives had become unmanageable.
2. Came to believe that a Power greater than ourselves could restore us to sanity.
3. Made a decision to turn our will and our lives over to the care of God as we understood Him.
4. Made a searching and fearless moral inventory of ourselves.
5. Admitted to God, to ourselves, and to another human being the exact nature of our wrongs.
6. Were entirely ready to have God remove all these defects of character.
7. Humbly asked Him to remove our shortcomings.
8. Made a list of all persons we had harmed and become willing to make amends to them all.
9. Made direct amends to such people wherever possible, except when to do so would injure them or others.
10. Continued to take personal inventory and when we were wrong promptly admitted it.
11. Sought through prayer and meditation to improve our conscious contact with God, as we understood him, praying only for knowledge of His Will for us and the power to carry that out.
12. Having had a spiritual awakening as the result of these steps, we tried to carry this message to alcoholics, and practice these principles in all our affairs. (Alcoholics Anonymous, 1976: 59-60)

Employee counselors or holistic employee assistance programs know about the local resources for their employees. Employers without these assistance programs should be aware that treatment modalities are much more successful than they used to be and that there is an AA group nearby and ready to address the needs of any employee troubled by alcohol addiction.

SUMMARY

As long as the mortality rate remains at 100 percent and perhaps until we find the fountain of youth, illness will always be among us. For each of us to claim responsibility for our wellness, however, and for employers to share the concern of health along with the medical profession seems to be the right and timely thing to do. It appears to some that the medical profession has, until recently, failed to embrace the concept of prevention as a fundamental concept. The dental profession has been articulating prevention for years, and it would appear that the average person born today in the United States will not have to be fitted with dentures. With proper brushing and flossing and with regular dental checkups, one should expect to live to a ripe old age with most of his or her teeth intact. Do you accept that you participate in your wellness?

When we assume a holistic model for health, and when we begin to practice a healthy and preventative lifestyle, a comprehensive shift toward wellness will follow. It is my premise that employers and employees in the workplace have the right, and perhaps the duty, to nudge psychergonomics along.

Chapter 4

Interconnected Wellness

There is an emotional component to every illness.

Karl Menninger

Your faith has healed you.

Matthew 9:22
The Living Bible

For the past twenty years I have been working diligently toward a holistic understanding of health and intentionally seeking ways to teach and facilitate this interconnected way of life. In the late 1970s and early 1980s, I found it frustrating that our culture, indeed the medical community, did not embrace what I acknowledged to be true. The emerging wellness clinics and holistic approaches to health, which among other things emphasized prevention as a meaningful concept, were regarded as newfangled and not in the mainstream of health care. Now, as we move into the twenty-first century, I am happy to say that these holistic ideas are now poised to be foundations of the new paradigm of health care. This readiness may have been more driven by employers and finances than philosophies or common practices, but it seems clear the data is available to energize the shift which must include replacing the concern for reimbursement with the concern for promoting wellness.

The nonholistic understanding of health is certainly not rooted in antiquity. Ancient writings by Greek philosophers, including Hippocrates (the father of medicine), did not segregate the many dimensions of one's being.

Perhaps it was the philosopher René Descartes in the seventeenth century who was initially influential in the separation of the fundamental mind, body, spirit dimensions of a person (Descartes, 1911). Descartes' intentional focus on the body "as if" the human were only physical set the stage for medical science to explode with information. However, the "as if-ness" was lost as the focus progressively became singular, that is, physical, in its scope. As the general practitioner progressively yielded to the medical specialties that emerged in the twentieth century, the discipline of health care seemed sufficiently dissected. Indeed, in some cases, the left-hand psyche did not know what the right-hand spirit was doing with the other appendages of the soma.

Today the concept of psychosomatic disease is hardly disputed. A stomachache, headache, or heartache can and often does manifest physically or in other dimensions of one's being. As a friend once said, "He is a real pain in the neck—it's good that I don't have a lower opinion of him." Certainly today, with the awareness of such things as hypnosis, biofeedback, spiritual direction, meditation, and placebos, one would have to be in denial to ignore the interconnected aspects that make one whole. Truly, homeostasis cannot be accomplished in any singular pursuit.

INTERCONNECTEDNESS

My first serious exposure to this interconnected way of understanding was through the writing of Heije Faber, a professor of psychology and religion from Holland, who offered attitudinal and behavioral symbolism in the mind-body-spirit triad (psychosomatic illnesses). In the final pages of his book, *Pastoral Care in the Modern Hospital* (1977), Faber contends that there are few illnesses that are not in some way affected by the personality and lifestyle of the sick person. Indeed, sickness is caused by an almost infinite array of possibilities with genetics being paramount. Yet, the mind-body-spirit link cannot be ignored. He offers four common illnesses and suggests how psychophysiological dynamics often mingle with, complicate, or even cause the illness.

Gastric ulcers are complicated by diet, and certainly antibiotics are the present way to eliminate these stomach-eating bacteria; yet, Faber cites other marked characteristics. Interestingly, the person with ulcers has a good intellect, a sense of orderliness, abundant energy, is independent, has a sense of duty, and has an oral emphasis. These people sometimes have to "stomach too much."

Asthma, of course, is affected by air quality and allergic reactions, yet such characteristics as being headstrong, egocentric, hot tempered, overly sensitive, and poorly integrated are often present. Asthma patients often "choke down their feelings."

Heart disease is clearly linked to poor diet, lack of exercise, smoking, and substance abuse. Those in the "coronary club" typically let their jobs come first, find it hard to say "no," seldom delegate responsibility, and usually find it difficult to relax—even at meals. Heart patients have too many "heartache" expressions.

Persons with *arthritis* have the common characteristics of being too controlled, pious, rigid, possessing a unique combination of fear and aggression and a strong "super ego." Their personalities are often called "stiff."

Our language is filled with volatile phrases that could be more appropriately expressed. It may be healthier to say:

"I found it awesome," instead of "I found it breathtaking."
"I felt emotional," instead of "I was all choked up."
"I am concerned," instead of "I have a heavy heart."
"This is disturbing," instead of "This will be the death of me."
"I like you," instead of "I'm crazy for you."
"It angers me," instead of "It makes me sick."
"I'm making sacrifices," instead of "I'm breaking my back."
"I'm feeling frustrated," instead of "I'm losing my mind."

Indeed, I could go on, but hopefully the point is made.

I remember visiting with a man in an intensive care unit and hearing him report on a major conflict that he and his wife were having shortly before his myocardial infarction. Toward the end of our visit, he said, "I guess I just take everything to heart." I asked, "Where do you take things?" I have seen many such situations where linguistic expressions find physical manifestations.

Well, of course, we cannot push this too far without becoming conscious of our own ailments and behavior. This awareness, however, is helpful in acknowledging subtle holistic relationships between mind, body, and spirit. Expressions such as, "He's driving me crazy," "You're dead wrong," "It took my breath away," "There's something I need to get off my chest," "That's getting under my skin," and "I'd die for that" are expressions that I eliminated from my speech, especially the statement, "She (or he) is killing me."

One of the current leaders in interconnected wellness is Louise L. Hay, who has written twenty books on the subject including the international best seller, *You Can Heal Your Life* (1984). In this book, Hay labels four negative emotions or attitudes that cause major problems in our bodies: resentment, criticism, guilt, and fear.

> Resentment that is long held can eat away at the body and become the disease we call cancer. Criticism as a permanent habit can often lead to arthritis in the body. Guilt always looks for punishment, and punishment creates pain. . . . Fear, and the tension it produces, can create things like baldness, ulcers, and even sore feet.
>
> I have found that forgiving and releasing resentment will dissolve even cancer. While this may sound simplistic, I have seen and experienced it working. (Hay, 1984, pp. 6-7)

Hay has an extensive work connecting the mind and spirit to the health of the body. In *Heal Your Body* (1982), Hay lists several hundred ailments, provides a probable psychosomatic cause, and suggests healing affirmations for each illness that aid in developing new thought patterns. Her intent is not to negate the appropriate forms of medical intervention. Rather, she seems to be calling for a paradigm shift to include the awareness that we all have the ability to contribute to our own healing process by taking care of our bodies, having an appropriate and positive mental attitude, and by having strong spiritual connections.

Norman Cousins, in his popular book, *Head First: The Biology of Hope* (1989), references an abundance of medical research which shows that negative emotions such as hate, fear, despair, depression, and resentment may produce changes in the body chemistry and set the stage for intensified illness. Very few studies, however, investigated whether the positive emotions of purpose, determination, faith, love, and hope impacted biological states. If we have the power to make ourselves sick, could we also have the ability to make ourselves well? Cousins thought, "Yes." In this relevant book, he reveals that belief becomes biology. Cousins says, "The major advances in modern medical science give substance to the principle that the mind of the patient creates the ambiance of treatment. Belief becomes biology. The head comes first" (1989, 281).

The 1990 publication *Healthy People 2000: National Health Promotion and Disease Prevention Objectives* contains a comprehensive agenda organized into twenty-two priority areas for health. Almost every one is related to lifestyle. Not only are certain thought patterns healthier than others, clearly lifestyle either can enhance one's well-being or be destructive.

The *Healthy People 2000 Fact Sheet* revealed that 15 percent of the Healthy People 2000 objectives reached or surpassed the year 2000 targets (ODPHP, 2000). Death rates for children one to fourteen years of age have declined by 26 percent from the 1987 baseline to surpass the year 2000 target of 28 deaths per 100,000 population. Preliminary 1997 data indicate a death rate of 25 per 100,000 population for this age group. Progress toward the targets has been made for another 44 percent of the objectives making the pursuit toward *Healthy People 2010* promising.

Toward the end of the 1990s, as the development and structuring of *Healthy People 2010* was getting under way, focus groups heard conflicting feedback from stockholders regarding *Healthy People 2000*. Health departments wanted the *Healthy People* document to grow in size. Business and managed care, however, reported that the document was already overwhelming in size. What resulted was expansion from about 300 objectives to over 500 objectives and the creation of a smaller and more succinct set of information called the *Leading Health Indicators*. This set of *Leading Health Indicators* is intended to assess progress toward health goals as a nation and prompt public understanding at state and local levels as progress is made in the first decade of the twenty-first century.

WORDS HAVE POWER

Relevant to unhealthy attitudes and expressions are the unfortunate choice of words that are common in the philosophy and practice of the medical profession itself. Too often treatment is seen as warfare in that the illness, injury, or disease is seen as the enemy, and the treatment modality is viewed as weaponry in the assault of the enemy. This is all well and good if the ill person (who becomes the battlefield) is charged with employing his or her "defenses" in the process, and other dimensions of the patient are not ignored or damaged.

Sticks and stones may break our bones, but words can be fatal. How many of us have heard the words: enemy, attack, invade, assault, bombard, warfare, kill, carnage, and magic or silver bullet in the context of medical care? How about, "We don't want to be too *heroic* in the beginning, but if the initial bombardment doesn't work, we will bring out the big guns." Whoa—wait a minute! The problem with using militaristic expressions and approaches is that the patient *is* the battlefield, and battlefields are seldom pretty sights. The phrase, "We attacked the cancer but the patient did not survive," comes to mind. Well, shame on that patient. That is not unlike, "The surgery was a success but the patient died."

Even though the alternative forms of medicine are each unique, they are typically respectful of the patient's inner, self-correcting forces that are seeking balance and wellness. Characteristically the alternative forms of care and treatment have in common the belief that health is a natural state and that this is acquired by being in harmony (not war) with all aspects of the self. Persons have within themselves the ability, when empowered, to accomplish the miraculous. Yet, when one is subdued and controlled, one is vulnerable indeed.

THE BODY SPEAKS

If in the process of medical care the illness is viewed apart from the message that it possesses, the message may be lost. If this is the case, and the symptom is removed before the message is understood, the ill person may unconsciously up the ante and become even more sick the next time. Medical care is not patient friendly if multidimensional homeostasis is not a part of the process.

If you have ever smoked, do you remember your first cigarette? There was a message in that initial cough. The translation goes something like this: "What? Are you leaving good judgment? This doesn't taste good and it burns the lungs!" If, however, one continued to ignore this message, the body would settle down until it said things such as, "This tastes good," or "I think I will have (need) another." Actually the body never stops sending messages. It is just that we learn to override the message and become numb to the signals.

When I was about fourteen years old, I saw a television commercial advertising a menthol brand of cigarettes. The picture showed a clear, cool river flowing over a waterfall. The message was that this brand was cool and refreshing. Well, it wasn't long until I purchased a pack of this minty-flavored smoke. My first inhalation felt like my head was blown off but because of other messages in our society, I ignored the one my body gave me.

Some of the messages within ourselves are not as blatant. Some of the messages are not in response to a substance. Yet, be it in response to an emotional stressor, a relational conflict, or a behavioral limitation the messages are flowing and balance is not achieved through ignoring them.

The late Franz Ingelfinger, while editor of the *New England Journal of Medicine,* reminded physicians that 85 percent of human illnesses are easily within the reach of the body's own healing system (1980). If this internal healing system is recognized and respected and not intentionally weakened through lifestyle, wellness would be the expected norm of our health.

Like many others, I used to believe that we were rather passive participants in our pursuit for health. I thought illness was an external force that caught us if we were in the wrong place (and sometimes if we were not). I thought that health was dispensed by doctors— through medicine and technology—in hospitals and medical offices. Certainly this myth has fed the sacred cow of the medical enterprise. Meaningful linguistic expressions such as, "I caught a cold," went right over my head. It is as if one had to go to great lengths, but "*I* finally caught it."

Holistic awareness allows us to realize that although medical doctors and technology play an important role in health care, a sizable portion of concern must return to the patient. Until now, it seemed that the loss of a monopoly is threatening to many doctors. Likewise, many patients are reluctant to assume such authority and responsibility. The fact is that the ultimate source of healing is within each of us, and to attempt to shift it elsewhere through reframing, threatening, and manipulating is neither going to change the reality nor enhance anyone's health. It is when we can embrace this idea and implement personal responsibility that we will be liberated to live with ourselves, in harmony with the planet and with one another. Until then, we will continue with a disease-care society and avoid participating in advocating and accomplishing a health care society. If we wait until our body speaks, we have waited too long. To rephrase President Kennedy's famous statement: "Ask not what outside entities can do about your health, ask what you can do for yourself."

AN INDUSTRY UNDER CHANGE

I believe that many people in the medical profession are frustrated with the current focus of wellness as well as the crisis in the health industry. Medical unions are being formed to fight the "big brother" control of HMOs and other forms of managed care. Yet, I am persuaded that most professionals have not lost the early calling and commitment to be a healer and to join the patient in this pursuit.

There are some, however, who claim that physicians have lost sight of their purpose and have lost themselves in the inner bowels of the medical enterprise. John Robbins, in his book *Reclaiming Our Health*, issues a stinging indictment on the medical system and particularly the American Medical Association (AMA) for growing impersonal, catering to special interests, and eliminating its competition instead of serving the health of the American people. In urging his readers to reclaim their health he states that:

> The medical paradigm that currently prevails in our society, and which the AMA stalwartly represents, has become so deeply entrenched that we often do not realize that it is simply one option among many. But there are other forms of medicine that represent different ways of understanding life and of promoting healing, and that, contrary to what the dominant medical establishment would have us believe, have demonstrated outstanding records of success. (1996, p. 227)

Throughout his book, Robbins offers many examples of alternative care which in some cases and in some countries provide better results than the conventional Western model of health care. Certainly, to suppress a mode of treatment that promotes health simply because it minimizes a monopoly or threatens a paradigm of operation, would be paramount to one religion trying to rid, destroy, or cleanse another. That falls short of the American ideal. Any form of treatment must take advantage of the body's natural tendency to want to heal itself. If intervention weakens the body through an abundance of pharmaceutical toxins, this natural tendency may be compromised. Through time, suppressive treatment may actually strengthen the disease instead of strengthening the body—as seen in developing resistant strains of viruses.

Moreover, it seems that the physicians of the twentieth century became the high priests of the Western world. To monopolize these dynamics and promote this belief to the neglect of recognizing and working with the healer within each of us is not unlike the high priests of yesteryear asserting that they alone were the dispensers of salvation. The religious protesters of the fifteenth and sixteenth centuries reopened the way for early Protestant Christianity to reclaim responsibility for spiritual authority. After all, how many of us remember having our temperature and blood pressure taken at the doctor's office and not being told what the readings were? Perhaps today, we stand at the threshold of claiming personal responsibility for our total well-being.

Just Imagine

During the 1970s innovative research with cancer patients was being done by O. Carl Simonton, MD, and Stephanie Matthews-Simonton, a motivational psychologist (Simonton, Matthews-Simonton, and Creighton, 1978). The Simontons utilized the traditional modes for cancer treatment—radiation, chemotherapy, and surgery—but also incorporated the use of imagery in their collection of treatment modalities. Initially (and perhaps like some today) their work was criticized for stretching beyond the accepted forms of medical care. Yet, once it was validated that many of their patients with cancer lived longer than expected, had more remissions, and dealt with pain better than others without the imagery—many took notice. The Simontons' imagery exercise involved patients creating a mental vision of their illness and picturing their white blood cells, their antibodies, or their entire immune system as positive healing forces and the cancer cells as the substance to be eliminated. The work that the Simontons accomplished validated to many of us the power that one dimension of our existence may have over another dimension of our being.

I remember once counseling a woman whose outlook on life was anything but positive. She obsessed about all the unfortunate circumstances befalling her. As one might expect, she also was experiencing a sundry assortment of physical ailments. I asked the woman to join me in a harmless mental exercise. "Picture," I said, "a large lemon on the table. Now I'm cutting it in half, and I want you to bite into it. Allow your mouth to be flooded with the fresh lemon juice."

"Wow," she said. "It's making my mouth water—and the glands in my neck are actually hurting."

"What?" I said. "Do you mean this playlike experience actually caused a physiological reaction?" This was a first step in revealing to her that imagined injustices were also playing themselves out in her in a holistic fashion.

When I was a child, we used to sing a song that went something like "the hip bone's connected to the leg bone, the leg bone's connected to the knee bone. . . ." Indeed, one's emotionality is linked to one's spirituality, which is entwined with one's physiology, and so it goes.

Why would we think that the effect of the placebo should operate in only one direction? A neutral prescription (tangible or otherwise) can shift toward wellness or illness. If people believe that it is going to help, it often does. If thinking is bent the other direction, the results are somewhat expected, yet, altogether unfortunate.

Positive Outlook

Another pioneer in the field of holistic health was Norman Cousins. His book *Anatomy of an Illness As Perceived by the Patient* (1979) revealed that attitude and optimism were paramount in the process of health. Cousins discovered that laughter is indeed good medicine. He had an illness that doctors did not believe to be reversible. Cousins reasoned that if negative emotions could set the stage for illness, then positive emotions might help set the stage for recovery. He found therapeutic value in hope, faith, love, cheerfulness, humor, playfulness, and creativity. He also learned the importance of maintaining a dialogue with the inner self, the doctor within, to strengthen his biological balance and enhance his immune system. In the 1970s and early 1980s it was interesting to learn of valid cases where basics such as laughter and vitamin C could improve health. Yet, in some ways, this information is still taught more than it is practiced.

SECONDARY GAINS OF ILLNESS

Case #1

A few years back, and in another state, I had a neighbor (I will call her Velma) who was a classic case in revealing the secondary gains of illness.

When I first met Velma, she was in her sixties and had endured twenty-two surgeries. I'm not sure what all of her surgeries involved, but I do know that many were of a major nature and some involved the removal of malignant tumors. Velma was married to an alcoholic, and she seldom, if ever, received affirmation and support from him. Since she was often sick, most of her thinking and conversation revolved around her unfortunate plight. Many of her neighbors considered her a hypochondriac and a negative personality. Consequently, she was avoided by almost everyone. There were exceptions, however. When Velma was deathly sick, members of the community and her church rallied in support. People visited her in the hospital. Her pastor prayed for her. Members of her church held her hand. Even her husband seemed to sober up. These endeavors were very costly (in every way) and yet, they always gave Velma what she so desperately needed: recognition and tender, loving care.

Attention and affirmation is a must for everyone if they are to experience fullness of life and wholeness in health. The obvious question is "Why or how could someone legitimately orchestrate their illness in this manner?" Consciously one does not, but it seems that if the fundamentals, acceptance from self and others, are missing, then one unconsciously creates circumstances whereby the fundamentals are achieved. Even a first-grader unconsciously knows that negative attention is better than no attention at all. The whole notion of secondary gains from an illness is a scary prospect, but it is one that cannot be ignored if we are to proceed holistically.

When one observes those who display habits detrimental to health, questions naturally arise. Does illness serve a function in and of itself? Is it meaningful that I am sick now? Well, with examples beyond that of Velma, I think it does. If illness only occurred in random fashion, there would be no need to emphasize lifestyles and healthy choices. Indeed bad things happen to good people, but also, bad habits lead to bad health. I am in no way suggesting a magic formula that would connect illness in general to the lack of a desire to be well. Most all of us are ill from time to time. Sometimes when illness happens, one may be unconsciously wrestling with issues of irresponsibility or perhaps the body may be saying, "If you don't slow down, I will make you slow down."

Case #2

Another scenario may ring familiar to many readers. Bill is a busy professional and has a schedule that tends to dictate his activities much of the day on most days. Bill notices that Tuesday of next week is presenting a very light schedule in his pocket dictator. Bill now starts to (perhaps even unconsciously) protect these blanks on Tuesday's calendar by scheduling more appointments on Thursday and going to the following Tuesday, if possible. As the Monday of the next week arrives, Bill notices that he feels exhausted, weak, and achy. On Tuesday morning, Bill notices that he doesn't quite fit his skin but has not clearly declared himself sick. He calls his secretary and learns that an important business meeting has just been announced and his presence is necessary and expected. Bill showers, puts on a crisp, white shirt, and departs for work looking great. His schedule led him as he led others, and before he knew it, it was 6 p.m. and he was ready to go home. The thought of how he felt at 7:30 a.m. was forgotten.

Now let's project three weeks into the future and the exact scenario presents itself again. This time when Bill calls his secretary early on Tuesday morning, nothing new seems to have arisen at work. Now with a voice that is raspy, he informs his secretary that he isn't feeling well. "Bill, you don't sound good at all," is the reply. Bill commits and informs the secretary that he will be taking a sick day. "OK, I think you should, Bill. You sound terrible. Take care of yourself and be sure to drink lots of fluids." Now, Bill is sick. Seeking objective data he checks his temperature—100.2 degrees. Now it's official. Bill stays reclined most of the day, follows normal protocol for this level of sickness, and amazingly is back to work on Wednesday. What a trooper! Now the important question—sound familiar?

Case #3

Parents of college students see this phenomenon more often than they would like. The story of Sally is classic. Sally is a nineteen-year-old college student who is vivacious and intent on experiencing all that life has to offer. She was an above-average student in high school, but now with no one enforcing structure, she tends to push the boundaries and test the limits. She is taking fifteen hours of credits, and two classes are suffering. Her part-time job is "cramping her style," and her credit card bill came in maxed with late fees. Midterms are next week, an unfinished paper was due last week, and Dad has left three messages on her voice mail. Sally, now finding herself with problems she cannot solve, notices that her emotional distress is being felt physically. She goes to the medical dispensary and gets it confirmed—Sally is sick!

"What about your classes and grades?" Dad asks Sally.

"I can't help it, Dad; I'm sick."

"What about your job and your bills?" asks Mom.

"I can't help it, Mom; I'm sick and need to come home."

This scenario is likely to repeat itself a few more times until Sally acquires the maturity to see farther down life's path than just the next moment and appreciate the forces of cause and effect. There is even a danger, if Sally continues to play out this unconscious game plan, that a future sickness could be quite serious.

Case #4

There is a classic story in the Gospel of John that captures one of these issues. According to the story there was a man who had an illness for thirty-eight years that left him unable to walk. Legend held that if one with an infirmity got into the water first, after the waters were disturbed, he or she would be healed. Jesus encountered this man and asked a very poignant question: "Would you like to get well?" (John 5:6 TLB). Interestingly, the man did not say "yes" or "no," but began to make excuses of how others always got to the water first. The question seems to be a critical one because initially it seemed as though he did not want to be made whole. Could not the removal of this man's infirmity also take away his concept of entitlement? Would not he need to be a responsible citizen if he were well? Could not it be a scary perspective to have to go where he had not gone and do what he had not done in thirty-eight years?

Case #5

A similar case was recently revealed in my office. Rose is a very intelligent and dynamic woman who, about thirteen years ago, experienced the untimely death of her twelve-year-old brother. Even though his death was the result of an unexpected brain aneurysm and was something that Rose could not have prevented, even if she were a medical doctor, she felt responsible. Guilt was ever present. Consequently, she struggled with depression and anxiety. Through time a sundry of ailments was upon her and she was considered by many to be "fragile." Through the years this behavior became her lifestyle. Extreme physical exertion was out of the question because she tired so easily. Because of this, Rose was exempt from the many strenuous activities that life often demands. As Rose came to terms with her brother's death, she then had to come to terms with a lifestyle that cut short the full experiences of her being. After a recent surgery which eliminated her most recent problem, she had to make a choice to replace this illness with another or go on with life. Her choice was for life. To her surprise, this choice carried with it an exhilarating sense of excitement. It was as though Rose was born anew. As she sought to express this newness of life, I asked her to try to capture her experience in writing. Below are her insightful and eloquent words.

> I have been ill in varying degrees for about thirteen years. I am twenty-seven, so now it seems that I am truly a new woman. Recently I had surgery, and I have the opportunity to be healthy.
>
> Having been ill for so long, I also suffered from depression, anxiety, and little confidence that "things would be okay." I knew that bad things happen to good people, and I was not immune. With this perspective, I struggled with decreased capacity for productivity and progression. I felt like I was trapped in mediocrity, that I might not get the chance to fulfill some basic goals and dreams. I was stuck in getting through the hour, the day.
>
> Even in this depressed state, there was the comfort that other people's expectations of me were lowered, out of necessity. I could say that's all I can do, and it was acceptable. (This took many years to get to that point.)
>
> Now I am standing on the threshold of health, of wellness, and it is both exciting and terrifying. I feel a personal responsi-

bility to grab this opportunity and run with it. At the same time, the fear of failure in my goals is stifling. I used to have a valid reason for taking it easy on myself, or praise that I tried. As a healthy person, that crutch has to be grown out of. I'm torn, because my attachment to my crutch helped me through so many hard times. Helen Keller was an inspiration to me. She said, "I cannot do everything, but I can do something. I will not refuse to do the thing which I can do."

My horizon is expanding. My affinity for this remarkable woman can't end with the "end" of my illness. . . . My abilities can be extended. If I refuse to act on this, it won't be long before my flexibility will decrease. I believe that I have been given another chance to redefine my self and my boundaries. The hurdle is to muster the courage to believe in myself; to balance my new life so mind, body and spirit are integrating.

It is a great gift and opportunity. It is too precious to me to let it pass by.

Because of Rose's resolve, I have great confidence in her ability, not only to stay well, but also to enthusiastically embrace life.

AFFIRMATION, ACCEPTANCE, AND WELLNESS

The pioneering work of Thomas Harris, MD, and Eric Berne, MD, in the field of transactional analysis has revolutionized the understanding of relationships and individual behavior. Harris contends that events such as birth and death are more of a process than we acknowledge, and certainly the birthing process is multifarious (Harris, 1973). Herein, Harris offers four births from conception to age five.

Cellular birth occurs at the point of conception, *physical birth* begins with breathing, *psychological birth* originates from "stroking," and *social birth* starts in school. The concept of the psychological birth and stroking is certainly germane here. *Stroking,* be it literal or otherwise, is essential to survival. A *stroke* may be used as the fundamental expression of social action—a unit of social intercourse. Psychologist Claude M. Steiner, a close collaborator with the late Eric Berne in the development of transactional analysis, suggests that stimulus hunger (as is satisfied through strokes), has the same relationship to survival to the human organism as food hunger. Steiner states, "Strokes are as necessary to human life as are other primary biological needs such as food, water, and shelter—needs which if not satisfied will lead to death" (1974, pp. 131-132).

The psychological community has known this information for years. The religious community incorporates this in the practice of worship, which means, "worth-ship." Certainly, it is not new to this writer. However, when it comes to the incorporation of this wisdom into the importance of health and wellness, it seems to be missing.

It is worthy to note that the unconscious ledger of stroke exchanges begins when life begins. Erik Erikson (1968) suggests that the first of the eight stages of human development is "trust versus mistrust." In this stage, the infant can neither converse nor interpret speech, yet profound truths are learned nonetheless. In fact, fundamental lessons are acquired that will go with the child all of his or her life. During this stage, the mother has a primary role, and communication between mother and child takes many forms. To the child, the authority of the mother is total. This is sensed, and implications are drawn from the outset. Mother can hear the baby cry and basically understand what that cry means. Does the cry imply pain, hunger, loneliness, or perhaps the need for a dry diaper? If the mother concludes that the baby is wanting to be fed and it is fifteen minutes until feeding time, she has the power to make the baby wait. The child senses this awareness and infantile interpretations are made. These early perceptions lead to conclusions wherein issues of trust and mistrust begin to be formed. "Can I trust that she (authority) will be here for me when I need her?"

Erikson's second stage of "autonomy versus shame and doubt" is also important here. The radius of significant others for the toddler now includes the father in the ranks of total authority. Relevant to this discussion is the importance of dad being available during this stage. If dad is physically present yet emotionally absent, the child may grow up with an insecurity of other authority figures' assistance and support. Also, if the father is punitive and wrathful, the child may likewise assume that others will be judgmental and legalistic. A sense of autonomy and individuation is highly preferred over shame and doubt when it comes to optimal health.

Each stage of human development has a psychological crisis whereby one may surface more on the positive side of the issue. Of course, the opposite is also true. To have an impression of self-worth, to trust and have a sense of integrity which is intact, one can lean into life with themes of grace, creativity, and health. One is never too old, nor does one outgrow the need to be recognized, affirmed, and accepted. In a word, *strokes* are the fuel of one's life force.

The reader may remember the motherless monkeys experiment (Harlow, 1959) where newborn monkeys were separated from their mothers and reared in cages with two artificial mothers. One artificial mother was made of wire with a rubber nipple from which the young monkey could get milk. The other mother type had no nipple for milk, but was made of soft, comfortable terry cloth. If attachments form entirely from the provided food, the baby monkeys would be expected to prefer the wire mother. What happened, however, was that the monkeys preferred spending their time with the soft mother. Especially when the infants were frightened, they clung to their terry cloth facsimile. Harlow concluded that the monkeys were motivated by the need for contact and comfort—not an alien concept for most humans.

Few things bring this truth home like the often referred to linguistic experiment of Frederick II. Reuben Fine references this story from Salimbene's *Thirteenth Century Chronicle* (1988). It seems that Duke Frederick wanted to find out what manner of speech children would have when they grew up if no one spoke to them before they acquired speech. Frederick ordered several newborn babies to be taken from their mothers and given to surrogate mothers who were to feed and clothe them, but never to talk or give communicative attention to them. All of the babies died. Of course, autopsies were not performed to determine the causes of death, yet this says to many that the babies died for lack of recognition and affirmation—for lack of strokes.

I believe that any of us who fall considerably short of the required strokes will, if not die, certainly become ill. Conversely, for any of us to grow and successfully overcome the stresses of life, we need more than just a maintenance portion of life-giving strokes.

With a health care industry that focuses on illness and disease, sizable portions of resources are directed toward after-the-fact remedies. Traditionally, medical scientists have studied the ill person and experimented with what substances or procedures helped and what did not. Specific diseases have been analyzed and consequences have been predicted. One of the things that the AIDS exigency taught us is that the best way to not die from AIDS is not get AIDS. This needs to be the lesson with all illnesses.

This is not to imply, however, that health is necessarily problem or disease free. To "heal" means to become "whole." I am at this moment thinking of someone, very close to me, who has cancer. This notwithstanding, he is the most whole person I have ever known. When a health crisis occurs, it often leaves one vulnerable. Wholeness allows the susceptibility for change to shift in the direction of wellness. The mortality rate is 100 percent. Ideally, wellness can be too.

PROACTIVE FOR WELLNESS

Psychergonomics takes the awareness of wellness and illness, which has been available to the health care industry for years, and seeks to make it relevant for business and industry through holistic counseling programs in the twenty-first century. Even though the paradigm of health care is shifting, I see the medical establishment moving at a snail's pace with the integration and implementation of this awareness. For instance, we know that we can often avoid a breakdown (illness) in our body by being preventative (healthy) in our lifestyle. The current thinking is that we can avoid *costly* treatment after the fact if we *invest* in maintaining optimal mind-body-spirit health. To further ensure this, we must realize that the body is not just a machine in good or bad repair but a dynamic multidimensional system that finds existence and meaning in family, friendships, work, community, and environment. The no-brainer expression, "The best way to stay healthy is not to get sick," is not just a trite statement, however. One must be proactive on the wellness side of this equation for it to be accomplished. Prevention of illness is dependent upon and synonymous with wholeness in relationships, vocation, recreation, diet, and goals—emotionally, physically, and spiritually. Health is influenced by what we physically ingest, the thoughts we have, the behavior we manifest, and the negative substances, emotions, and attitudes that we fail to eliminate.

When all of the systems of the body are operating in a balanced and efficient way, the body assumes its desired condition of health. Even the regaining of homeostasis (healing) is a natural power. The Constitution of the World Health Organization (WHO) has this definition for health: "Health is a state of complete physical, mental, and social well-being and not merely the absence of disease or infirmity" (WHO, 1948).

Because of this awareness I offer these twelve psychergonomic principles of wellness.

Principles of Wellness

"Physical health is not merely the absence of physical illness, Mental health is not merely the absence of mental illness and Spiritual health is not merely the absences of spiritual illness."

1. Illness is a process and not an event—so is wellness.
2. Illness is a metaphor of what is wrong in one's life and is filled with meaning.
3. Meaningful and purposeful existence promotes health.
4. Acceptance and affirmation is as critical to health as diet and exercise.
5. Linguistic expressions often find physical manifestations in getting sick.
6. There are sometimes unconscious secondary gains in getting sick.
7. Disease in one dimension of a person's life may present itself in another dimension.
8. Illness does not occur in just one part of a person's life.
9. Enhancement in one part of a person's life leads to improvement in other parts.
10. One can minimize the forces outside one's control, such as losses and carcinogens, by maintaining a healthy attitude and lifestyle.
11. The psyche is primary or coequal in all illness and wellness.
12. Everyone has a healer within.

Chapter 5

Mind–Body–Spirit

Yet, as has been indicated, ALWAYS will it be found that the ATTITUDE of the mental forces of a body finds its inception in those things that come into growth; for what we think and what we eat - combined together - MAKE what we ARE; physically and mentally.

Edgar Cayce
Reading number T0288-038 F

Health is contagious.

Howard Clinebell
Anchoring Your Well-Being

All of us hold a position in the ranks of the walking wounded. Be it a childhood wound, a death of a loved one, a recent divorce, a relationship in conflict, financial pressures, a physical ailment, or emotional difficulties. The next person that you encounter will not likely have the same wounds that you have, neither will this person display personal wounds openly. Be assured, however, that everyone is struggling with some issue to some degree. Do not think that these wounds do not impact wellness. To be able to identify these difficulties and appropriately manage them has everything to do with interconnected wholeness.

When I speak of wholeness (or interconnected wellness) the reference is to the traditional inclusion of mind, body, and spirit. Many references to wholeness will cite these three dimensions specifically. I want to say here, however, that wholeness also involves such fundamentals as nature and environment, culture and institutions, work and play, and relationships and community. Wholeness is impacted by such variables as economy, climate, perception, and crisis. Every dimension of a person and his or her holistic components touches and overlaps all of the other dimensions. Wholeness involves dynamic energy, never static, always in ferment and refinement, achieving growth and balance. Having said this, allow the expression of wholeness to be fundamentally embraced with the tripartite reference to mind, body, and spirit.

MIND

> If a patient could promote the healing process from within, that would be the cure for cancer.
>
> Deepak Chopra
> *Quantum Healing:*
> *Exploring the Frontiers of Mind/Body Medicine*

To consider health apart from the mind would be like trying to calculate the volume of a space without one of the dimensions of height, width, or depth. I am of the opinion that the mind is not just housed in the brain but would like to suggest that the mind represents intellect, conscious and unconscious processes, as well as thoughts, perceptions, intuitions, and emotions. Mental wellness is indicated by such things as self-acceptance, realistic self-perception, differentiation of self, control of impulses, a sense of responsibility, empathy, and an inner security. All of these factors, of course, wax and wane with life's ebb and flow. Yet, that which is hoped for, committed to, and empowered toward wellness is not lost. Ideas, attitudes, memories, perceptions, feelings, and beliefs play a significant role in wellness. So do such things as chronic anger, fear, guilt, depression, lack of forgiveness, powerlessness, and self-rejection.

We are, in part, the result of what we think and what we fail to eliminate. What we fail to eliminate in a physical sense is important. The elimination processes of bowel and bladder remove toxins, as do other glands and organs of the body. Yet to fail to eliminate negative and undesired emotions and attitudes will contaminate the system as well. Even the releasing of the bondage of a compulsion, be it to a schedule, neatness, diet, drugs, ritual, or sexual obsession, can be a totally liberating experience.

If a negative mind-set, unresolved anger, lingering guilt, and despair produces adverse physiological changes, doesn't it stand to reason that hope, faith, purpose, and love will bring beneficial changes to one's health?

The power of the mind seems to have always been recognized in the professions that are concerned with wellness. Unquestionably, the medical community seeks to harness this force with the use of placebos. There are some that give the placebo effect no more power than the inactive substance that it contains. If the understanding of the placebo is held in pejorative terms, its potency will not be fully recognized. However, when the effect is recognized as an expression of the doctor within, healing processes may result from a neutral substance, lifestyle changes, doctor-patient interaction, or other ritualistic procedures.

In many ways, the major religions of the world give credence to the individual's ability to participate in his or her wellness. The Judeo-Christian proverb, "As he thinketh in his heart, so is he" (Proverbs 23:7), captures this awareness. There are those in the religious community that seem more bent on guilt and condemnation than acceptance and wholeness, yet, many proceed with a desire to bless and make whole. Certainly this theme is embraced by those like Norman Vincent Peale who recognize the power of positive thinking.

This awareness is fundamental to the profession of psychology. Such things as stress, burnout, and post-traumatic stress disorder are clearly related to health. Being attentive to external factors, such as environment and support systems, and internal factors, such as epistemology and coping skills, are crucial to wellness. A psychotherapist may realize that there are times where an unconscious technique may result in greater improvement to overall health than a psychological intervention that consciously seeks to educate and heighten one's awareness of cause and effect.

Interventions such as hypnosis offer undisputed examples of the power of the mind. Hypnotic suggestions have been used to modify behavior and manage pain. Such uses as weight reduction, smoking cessation, chronic pain management, and childbirth are common. Self-hypnosis is as appropriate an idea for some as is meditation. Athletes, whose performance is rated in hundredths of a second, find that self-hypnosis and imagery may give them the edge they need. Those who compete at the Olympic level have been utilizing hypnosis for years. They not only use hypnosis and visualization to improve their performance through their mind; they also picture themselves as progressively healthy and injury free.

For me to say that I can control the temperature in my hands through mental effort may sound somewhat mystical. However, to understand that one form of biofeedback does just that, we may begin to appreciate that there is a method to the process. Biofeedback is a therapeutic modality that gives clinical feedback on such bodily responses as skin temperature, muscle activity, and brain waves. Through special mental exercises and autogenic phrases one learns specific control as well as an overall self-regulatory pattern. Through instant feedback, one can learn how mental processes, feelings, and thoughts affect the body. Divers learn how to slow the body's metabolism and lower the need for oxygen, shamans can lower their heart rate to a phenomenally low level, and clinical uses include pain management, stress reduction, and other forms of somatic control.

In 1995 I set out on the ambitious goal of running what was to be my first full marathon. My running partner and training guru, Phil, told me that the effort required between miles 16 and 21 would be physically taxing beyond what I had ever experienced before. Between miles 21 and 26.2 would be an experience of mental endurance. How right he was. The physiological changes that occurred in my body were unlike anything I had experienced before. My body said stop, and every stride called for resources beyond what were there physically. I imagined that I was running on air and envisioned that I was riding a horse. I knew these were mental tricks, but I needed help in every way I could fathom. Yes, my training had brought me to the level of running a marathon, but I did not appreciate all that Phil had prepared me for until I was about three miles from the finish line. I had proven my physical ability up to then—it was my mental preparation that carried me through.

Some of the most convincing research revealing a correlation between how the mind affects the body was done in the 1960s. The pioneering efforts of Thomas Holmes and Richard Rahe, of the University of Washington School of Medicine, developed a standard by which stress could be calculated and its effects measured. Holmes and Rahe, with a working assumption that all change, positive and negative, is stressful, engaged over 5,000 people to determine what life events were more demanding that others (Holmes and Rahe, 1967b). From this study, Holmes and Rahe created the Social Readjustment Rating Scale. This test score revealed one's level of stress and potential threat to the person's well-being (Holmes and Rahe, 1967a). Such life events as death of a spouse, divorce, illness, marriage, major mortgage, vacation, and Christmas were assigned a numerical value. Some of the life adjustments within a given year were to be expected, yet some, of course, were unwelcome. Some were positive and others were negative. All involved change. The interesting findings, however, suggested that the higher the score, the greater the risk for getting sick. In fact, a score of 300 or greater (out of a possible score of nearly 1,500 points) could threaten well-being. Most of the life adjustment events found on this test are normal life occurrences. It is when one gets overwhelmed with the accumulation of stressors that dangerous stress reactions take place. It is then that one must seek to take charge of the things that are under one's control and look for ways to minimize change.

Tranquilizers are consumed at an alarming rate in our society. The reason that tranquilizers are near the top of the list of prescriptions written by the typical physician is because they work. Tranquilizers reduce, if not eliminate, the response to disturbing outside stimuli. The pills do not change the environment, only our reaction to it. I am convinced that tranquilizers have a place in our society; yet, I also believe that they can screen us from appropriate problem solving. On the one hand, they may temporarily deflect the need to respond to a situation that won't go away on its own, and on the other hand they may prevent people from learning the necessary skills to overcome life's difficulties. An endongensis tranquilizer is employed in Reinhold Niebuhr's prayer that is voiced in Alcoholics Anonymous (AA) meetings across our land: "God, grant me the serenity to accept the things I cannot change, courage to change the things I can, and the wisdom to know the difference."

BODY

Just as bees transform medical herbs into sweet honey, so in life when the heart is leavened with compassion, it becomes full of joy.

A plaque in the Garden of the Leavened Heart
Greenfield, Michigan

The physical body is a symphony of systems working in orchestration to achieve balance and health. The body is designed to operate in homeostasis and yet is also prepared to regain it when lost. Even the word *health* is derived from the Old English *hale,* which means whole. Not only is the body affected by such things as belief and perception, as well as environment and nature, the multifarious subsystems within the body are ever working to maintain wholeness.

Consequently, every physical substance that enters the body makes an ultimate difference in the degree of wellness experienced. This of course includes what one ingests in the form of food, but also includes what one inhales, absorbs, injects, or manufactures within the body. Substances from the body's internal apothecary are constantly in adjustment to meet the demands in the wonderful experience we call life.

There are about 100 neurotransmitters that transfer information across synapses to accomplish the chemical communications that help keep the body informed and balanced. The phrase "chemical imbalance" is usually a reference to one or more of the seven most important neurotransmitters: acetylcholine, norepinephrine, serotonin, dopamine, GABA, glutamate, and endorphins. These chemicals affect bodily functions such as movement, memory, sleep, learning, mood, appetite, and aggression. They may be associated with such disorders as Alzheimer's disease, depression, Parkinson's disease, schizophrenia, and epilepsy. Of relevance here is that the loss of homeostasis can be cyclical and the cause and effect so intertwined that it may be almost impossible to determine what is acting and what is being acted upon. It can be the classic "What came first, the chicken or the egg?" dilemma. In many cases, as is indicative of systems, it is a both/and scenario. Having a chemical imbalance may imply that undesired effects (such as depression) are a singular result of the imbalanced chemistry. Such hasty conclusions do not take into account a systemic and holistic view of the body. One may also conclude that the chemistry is off because of an internal or external stressor (be it physical, emotional, or spiritual), and the trauma is further complicated by such things as perception and support. For one to lose a spouse in death will in many cases disrupt chemical balance. There may even be a need for drug therapy. Yet, since an event triggered the imbalance, intervention to regain the balance must also include holistic approaches that addresses the event itself and the adjustments necessary to cope with the loss. Consequently, psycho-therapy and antidepressants are usually indicated in tandem for depression.

The body has a wisdom that is far beyond our ability to fully appreciate. Every gland and organ has a purpose and in working with all the systems of body seeks to accomplish its function. Fortunately, surgeons equipped with this information are not as quick to remove tonsils and adenoids today as they were when many of us were children.

The human body consists of about 50 trillion cells, and each of those fulfills a special function. Cloning has revealed that each cell contains the blueprint for duplicating the totality of a body—down to the color of eyes or hair. This raises the intriguing question, "Just where does the mind reside?" Certainly if the information for the size of one's ears can also be found in a cell in one's big toe, can we conclude that the mind is only in the head?

As the nervous system provides information about what is going on inside and outside one's body and facilitates an appropriate response, and the endocrine system coordinates the internal world regulating functions from stress responses to physical growth, the immune system serves as both a sensory system and a surveillance system. The immune system monitors the internal state of the body and detects unwanted cells and toxins that potentially disrupt the body's balance. This doctor within was revealed to me as a little boy when my parents took me to the country doctor. Doctor Duvalt told my parents that is was a good thing that they brought me in for the "shot." With the treatment he expected me to get well in about seven days. Without the shot, it may have taken me a full week to recover, suggesting that the body has its own forces of healing.

The immune system eliminates or inactivates foreign substances in the body such as viruses, bacteria, and cancer cells. There is a direct correlation between a weakened immune system and getting sick. In fact, disabling the immune system is the process by which the human immunodeficiency virus (HIV) leads to AIDS and leaves the HIV-infected person defenseless against opportunistic infections and cancers.

A relatively new discipline in health care is psychoneuroimmunology. Psychoneuroimmunology, as the name implies, is the study of the synthesis of the psyche or mind, the brain and nervous system, and the body's cellular defenses against abnormal internal cells and external agents such as bacteria and viruses. In fact, without a treatment of cure for AIDS, the treatment has advanced extensively thanks in part to the discipline of psychoneuroimmunology.

There is a sense in which the body is ultimately strengthened when the immune system is engaged in defense. Just as broken bones typically become stronger than before, and scar tissue is tougher than similar tissue that was not damaged, the immune system adapts an innate ability to be prepared against certain bacteria and viruses the second time around. Fortunately, because of the immune system's ability to prevail over foreign intruding agents, and the ability to remember how to eliminate these agents, we get sick from certain illnesses only once. In some cases, such as smallpox, one can be inoculated by the virus in such small amounts that the immune system becomes ever vigilant over the spread of the virus.

The body's overall system even becomes tolerant of the common and familiar microscopic "bugs" found in the household. These are friendly germs—they are family germs that grew up with the family and the family with them. Therefore, family members typically develop immunity to these potentially harmful critters. To experience the unfamiliar germs of another family may prove to be not so friendly. This is precisely what happens when U.S. residents go to Mexico and experience "Montezuma's Revenge." These germs don't seem to bother the Mexicans. They are used to them. In fact, the familiar diseases of the Europeans proved to be devastating to the Native Americans as the Europeans progressively came to this continent with germs that the Native Americans were ill prepared for.

Interestingly, many diseases, among them diabetes, rheumatoid arthritis, and cancer, have the cause of the disease around us or within us all the time. Most people have malignant cells and many have the rheumatoid factor, yet, relatively few of us are diagnosed with these diseases. Clearly our immune systems and other forces of health and wholeness are at work.

Because of this awareness, Larry Dossey, while speaking at the 1999 American Association of Pastoral Counselors Convention in Albuquerque, New Mexico, said (and I am paraphrasing): "For parents to accomplish the feat of sheltering their children from all childhood diseases, would in essence set their children up for sudden death upon becoming an adult." We can be grateful that childhood diseases such as the mumps are usually endured at an early age and never experienced again. One may appreciate that he or she is stronger because of such things as measles, mumps, and chicken pox.

Perhaps one of the greatest examples of the holistic nature of the body can be illustrated in a set of responses known as the fight-or-flight phenomenon. Harvard physiologist Walter B. Cannon (1932) was the first to describe this response early in the twentieth century. The late Hans Selye followed this research at McGill University where he demonstrated that the human body reacts to modern stresses as if experiencing a real physical threat (1950).

Fight-or-flight is a series of electrical and biochemical responses that occur in response to a threat. This afterburner effect provides a burst of energy that in the course of the response (fight-or-flight) is expected to be burned off. The problem is, even though the instinct served our caveman ancestors very well in terms of responding to the threat of an animal or someone from another tribe, the world now presents threats of a more ambiguous and psychological nature. How does one run away from or stay and fight the intangible and indirect threats resulting from conflicted relationships, financial problems, and the rapid pace of change? Yet, since the chemicals need to be burned off as if physical exertion had been engaged, the whole response points to the need for aerobic exercise as the means to eliminate these chemicals. It seems that social evolution has gotten one step ahead of the body's adaptive response in this regard. Yet holistically, one can intellectually realize there are times when exercise is beneficial and realize there are times when exercise is essential.

Kenneth R. Pelletier, a senior clinical fellow at the Stanford Center for Research in Disease Prevention, offers a thorough summary of physiological sequence of events involved in fight-or-flight in his book, *Mind As Healer, Mind As Slayer.* Specifically, Pelletier says:

> All of us are familiar with the feeling of a sudden flush of excitation or an "adrenaline rush." This occurs when the adrenal medulla releases its stress hormones and causes the entire body to respond with a jolt and a tremendous surge of energy. Such a reaction sometimes enables people to perform feats of physical strength that they would not normally be able to do, such as when a wife lifts an automobile to save her trapped husband. The whole system enters a state of hyperactivation in which the heart races, body temperature rises, oxygen consumption increases. There are subtle differences in the quality of this fight/

flight reaction, which occur as a result of the differential secretions of the adrenals. Two secretions of the adrenal medulla, adrenaline and noradrenaline, serve different purposes, and the proportion in which they are released is controlled in a feedback loop by the hypothalamus through the sympathetic nervous system. Adrenaline acts through the liver and mobilizes glucose into the bloodstream, providing a quick source of energy for cells to metabolize in response to stress. Adrenaline also increases carbohydrate metabolism, dilates the arterials of the heart and skeletal muscles, accelerates heart rate and increases the volume of blood the heart circulates through the body, elevates body temperature, and increases oxygen consumption and carbon-dioxide production. Additionally, it acts to relax the smooth muscles of the gastrointestinal tract while producing constriction of the sphincter muscles, and it dilates the bronchial musculature. Shallow respiration and anus contraction are among the subjective components of this reaction.

. . . Both adrenaline and noradrenaline cause an increase in circulating free fatty acids. There is a discernible difference between proportions of adrenaline and noradrenaline released from one stress response to another. The reasons why adrenaline is released in one instance and noradrenaline in another are not clearly understood, but many researchers tend to regard adrenaline as the "fear hormone" and noradrenaline as the "anger hormone." In other words, a differentiation that can be clearly classified as psychological in nature seems to be the decisive factor in determining how the adrenal medulla responds. (Pelletier, 1992, pp. 61-62)

The more the medical profession learns about the human body, the more the body is understood to be interdependent on and interconnected with systems within and beyond the skin. It is ironic that our society seems obsessed with fitness and appearance yet is simultaneously neglectful, if not abusive, of healthy choices and holistic involvement. As we seek to be attentive to issues of wholeness may we listen perceptively to our bodies and realize that before the body screams in pain, it whispers in discomfort. When we better learn to listen to and befriend our bodies, we will tap the body's wisdom and experience more comfort, pleasure, energy, and strength.

SPIRIT

A cheerful heart does good like medicine, but a broken spirit makes one sick

Proverbs 17:22
The Living Bible

When I was a teenager, I was able to fix just about anything that went wrong with my car. I worked inside engines, replaced transmissions, repaired dents, and removed squeaks. Problems and cars seemed to go together. Today I would not know how to change the points in my car even if my car had points. In fact, I don't have the computerized equipment to work on my car even if I had the know-how.

Medically, a similar paradigm shift has occurred. We take our bodies to repair shops (clinics or hospitals) where we may be hooked up to computer analyzers (CAT scans and MRIs). Where would we be without these diagnostic centers and angiograms and lithotripters? Now I am not knocking these advances. These are signs of our times. If it was determined that I needed a sonogram of my gizzard, of course, I would want this done (from both sides). My point is, are we just machines in good or bad repair? Or are we more?

I do not like it when my car breaks down, and I like it even less when my body breaks down. But is wellness (or wholeness) simply the absence of illness? Is wholeness only understood in terms of a finely tuned machine? Are the means to wholeness totally dependent on externals such as diet, exercise, medicine, surgery, and technological marvels? Again, I exercise and try to eat a balanced diet. Also, I draw comfort in my physicians' skills and tools. But our awareness of our spiritual dimension makes us more—much more. If we did not have a spiritual dimension, we would be perhaps more of a slave to external factors than we are.

Whether our bodies are sick or well, we are spiritual, and consequently, we are more. It sometimes seems as though the evangelistic fervor to save our souls found in the tent revivals of yesteryear are replaced with the secular quest to preserve our bodies found in the high-tech mind-set of our health-conscious society today. I suggest that if in so doing we miss attaining a state of grace and ignore participating in caring communities, our results are less than holistic.

If you are a pianist you may create harmony on the keyboard, but because of your spiritual dimension, you are the music. Your car may be in excellent repair, but because of your spiritual dimension, you are the journey. Your body may be in perfect physical condition, but because of your spiritual dimension, your potential is love and your result is wholeness.

This is important to me because I believe in the holistic nature of our being. Most people know they have emotions but too often fail to see how this is a part of their wellness. Most claim a spiritual awareness but fail to equate this with health. From my perspective, our multiple dimensions are one. Wholeness is a process resulting from nurturing all aspects of our being. Wholeness is a process resulting from congruence in the interconnectedness of our being.

When we become awestruck in the complexities of life with all of its mountain and valley experiences and celebrate the miracle of our existence, we are in the process of being whole. When we have a love affair with life, it is a spiritual experience that moves us toward wholeness even in the midst of life's challenges.

The apparent influence of the spiritual dimension seems to wax and wane—at least in the Western world. Currently, there seems to be a general discounting of rigid religious elitism. I would hasten to concur that any expression of pathology is not healthy. Yet, in terms of recognizing and articulating spiritual concepts and values, we seem to be experiencing a liberating freedom of expression.

A December 1994 Gallup Poll (Princeton Religion Research Center, 1996) revealed that belief in God in the United States has remained stable over the past fifty years, with 94 percent of younger U.S. residents (ages eighteen to twenty-nine) expressing belief and 97 percent of older adults (ages fifty or over) believing in God. The poll further indicated that 58 percent of all U.S. residents indicated that religion was very important in their lives with only 9 percent indicating that it was not important. The report shows that 43 percent had attended church or synagogue at least once within the past seven days. This makes religious participation the most common form of voluntary social activity in the United States—even greater than all sports activities combined.

There are about 350,000 congregations of all faith groups in the United States. The opportunity for religious organizations to assist in the promotion of wellness is profound. Not since religious groups led in the establishment of the first hospitals in the Middle Ages have churches and synagogues been poised to once again lead the course for wellness and wholeness. Congregations are the largest network of voluntary associations in the Western world.

The television and movie industry have many shows that speculate on the presence of higher powers and often convey messages of hope, endurance, and responsibility. Popular television shows such as *Touched by an Angel* and *Oprah* are subtly contributing to spiritual awareness. Recent movies such as *City of Angels* and *What Dreams May Come* tend to have themes that are redemptive. Who has not heard the phrase, "May the Force be with you"? These themes are not only prevalent in the entertainment industry, it is not uncommon for well-known people in business and varied professions to feel free enough to openly say, "I will be praying for you."

The profound work of The Foundation for Inner Peace in their book *A Course in Miracles* and the writings of such people as Deepak Chopra (in the field of medicine), Suze Orman (in the field of finance), Howard Clinebell (in the field of religion), Gary Zukov (in the field of frontier science), and Steven Covey (in the field of family and business), have positively influenced the acceptability of spiritual issues by being holistic in the understanding of their discipline. Assuredly people such as Marianne Williamson, Larry Dossey, James Redfield, Sarah Ban Breathnach, Bernie Siegel, M. Scott Peck, Harold Koenig, Wayne Dyer, Jeffrey Levin, Andrew Weil, and many others have also put spirituality in vogue.

I would certainly not attempt to minimize the Christian concept of the trinity by drawing simple comparisons to holistic principles. Yet, on the surface, the mind-body-spirit understanding can find resonance in the theology of the trinity.

It is when we can broaden our base and see the balance in the world, the congruence in the midst of incongruence, that we become aware that that which is physical is also spiritual and that which is spiritual is also emotional. Indeed energy in an instant becomes matter and light can take form.

Sarah Ban Breathnach discerns this as she captures this principle while working with her plants.

Leaf. Stem. Root.
Mind. Body. Soul.

Three in one. Spirit's seamless thread of mystery. I have often thought that if I could just discover where one strand left off and another began, I could understand it all. As it is, I understand little, yet somehow I know.

I set the plant into a slightly larger pot. Not too large; we must not overwhelm but encourage. So too, I must not take on the world but simply each task before me. Now I add rich potting soil. Water. Slowly I take the plant to a shady spot for a day so that it can become adjusted to its new environment. But even at this moment, the stem seems straighter, the leaves uplifted. "Speak to Him thou for He hears," Tennyson urges. Spirit with Spirit can meet—closer is He than breathing, and nearer than hands and feet."

Root and bud bear silent witness to the restoration. (1995, June 28)

Harold Koenig, MD, from Duke University has done extensive research (primarily at Duke University Medical Center) on religion and health. In a study of 836 persons over the age of sixty living in the Midwest, Koenig found that persons who frequently attended church and engaged in prayer and Bible reading experienced significantly higher well-being than those who were less religiously involved (1997). Spiritual and religious activity had positive outcomes with depression, anxiety, substance abuse, blood pressure, stroke, heart disease, cancer, and mortality. Koenig says, "While it may be true that those who are healthy are more able to attend church, this is not the whole story. Several of these studies have taken disability level into account and still found that the more religiously involved live longer" (1997, pp. 53-55).

Perhaps the grandest example giving credence to the presence of the spiritual is to reference some medical studies that seem to validate the power of prayer. One of the most famous studies on prayer was done with heart patients during the 1980s (Byrd, 1988). This was a controlled experiment with 393 patients in a modern hospital with the variable being praying for 192 of the patients and not for the other 201 (the control group). The prayed-for patients, unaware of the experiment, experienced significant and therapeutic results over the patients who were not targeted with prayer. In this double-blind experiment, the prayed-for patients were three times less likely to develop pulmonary edema and five times less likely than the others to require antibiotics.

Since then, scores of studies and researchers are validating, through the scientific method, what many have believed all along. Certainly at the forefront of this research is Larry Dossey, MD. Initially, Dossey was astonished that his literature research unearthed many studies that had not been incorporated into the knowledge or practice of the scientifically trained physician. At first surprised by the data, and later challenged, Dossey has dedicated much of his time and attention to the effects of prayer and has written extensively on the subject.

In one of his earlier books on prayer, *Healing Words* (1993), Dossey refers to the findings of Daniel J. Benor, MD, on spiritual healing. This work showed that prayer positively affected high blood pressure, wounds, heart attacks, headaches, and anxiety. Subjects went beyond humans to include such things as water, enzymes, bacteria, fungi, yeast, red blood cells, cancer cells, pacemaker cells, seeds, plants, algae, moth larvae, mice, and chicks. The positive results of prayer were not dependent on whether the praying person was in the presence of that which was being prayed for or far away. Indeed, nothing seemed capable of blocking this healing. For instance, when an object was placed in a lead-lined room or in a cage that shielded it from all known forms of electromagnetic energy, the effects still got through. With this kind of scrutiny, and the use of the double-blind method, Dossey believes that this rules out the effect of the placebo, the power of positive thinking, and hypnotic suggestion.

In fact, Dossey gradually reached a point where he resolved that to not use prayer in his practice was equivalent to withholding a potent drug or surgical procedure. In *Prayer Is Good Medicine,* Dossey says, "As a physician, I have employed medications and surgical procedures because I know they work. But prayer works, too" (1996, p. 5).

This kind of research is moving us leaps and bounds beyond the schizophrenia which has too often been present with science and religion. In both camps, the baby has sometimes been discarded with the bathwater and elements of truth ignored. As the spiritual-scientific world continues to reunite, there will be descendants who are *great healers.* The pursuit of recognizing and understanding these intertwined dynamics of mind, body, and spirit is indeed the pursuit of psychergonomics.

Chapter 6

Practicing Wellness

Whether you think you can or whether you think you can't, you're right.

Henry Ford

The biochemistry of the body is a product of awareness.

Deepak Chopra
Ageless Body, Timeless Mind

We are coming of age. According to our current calendar system, we are now twenty-one (centuries, that is). Hopefully, we are now prepared to move beyond our adolescent magical thinking, beyond snake oils, and beyond letting our bodies fall prey to some illness before assuming responsibility for our own wellness.

To achieve wellness, we must not only acknowledge and respect all the dimensions of our being heretofore mentioned, we must also recognize and utilize the network of systems within our communities, which also contribute to total health. We must be more collaborative with preventive and alternative forms of medical care. We must be allies with law enforcement to head off crime. We have to identify needy families and connect these situations with social services agencies. We need to be prepared to refer couples for credit counseling. We need to know valid centers that offer mental health counseling and substance abuse treatment. If the greatest agencies and resources in the nation are in our communities and we do not access them, how can they help?

Recently, I had a meaningful collaborative exchange with my physician. As I was doing a counseling session with a new employee, I discovered some medical issues that could not be ignored. The employee was also new to the area and had not yet acquired a personal physician. Understanding the importance of his medical need, I phoned my physician with the hope that my client could be seen. My doctor is unable to accept new patients, but because of our working relationship, he made an exception. The significant aspect of this case is how my physician went the extra mile with the new employee. When I saw the employee just two days later, he presented me a note from my doctor that thanked me for my initial intervention and provided some ingenious information that he had obtained regarding suitable support systems that we both knew the patient needed. This kind of professional respect and collaboration is essential in the realization of total well-being. Furthermore, getting to know one's doctor personally creates a rapport and dimension of respect that flows both ways. Doctors cannot get to know all of their patients, but I want my doctor to know me. To engage the resources at our disposal for the purpose of health is not only responsible, it is being holistic.

HEALTHY MODELS FOR WELLNESS

What if researchers also turned their attention to a group of people who represent prototypes of optimal health? What could be learned by studying those in the best of health instead of those who are in the worst of health? Well, someone has. Kenneth Pelletier in his Sound Mind, Sound Body Project (1994) focused on fifty-one individuals (twenty-one women and thirty men ranging in age from twenty-eight to ninety-six). Each of these persons met the criteria of being "prominent" in the sense that they were acknowledged by their peers as being accomplished in their chosen profession or businesses; they were recognized for overall good health and healthy practices; and either explicitly or implicitly, each participant conveyed the personal convictions that he or she possessed a deep sense of purpose and higher or spiritual values.

Pelletier's study revealed that such factors as childhood illnesses and trauma can strengthen the constitution and nurture the capacity to empathize. Unfortunate occurrences may awaken a deeper meaning that was jarred loose only by the crisis itself.

To have a sense of control was also a common theme that Pelletier discovered as an important factor in optimal health. The World Health Organization (WHO) further incorporates this concept in their definition of health, which is: "The extension to all peoples of the benefits of medical, psychological and related knowledge is essential to the fullest attainment of health" (WHO, 1948). Utilizing an optimistic understanding of control along with inner values, ethics, constraint, and compassion was present with all the participants in this study.

Finding and fulfilling a purpose was another factor in optimal health that the Sound Mind, Sound Body Project discovered. As the premier mythologist Joseph Campbell pointed to the need to "follow your bliss," and Abraham Maslow pointed to the plateau of "self-actualization," one must apply self-control in the here and now to accomplish the potential of tomorrow.

Other determinants such as a network of friends, philanthropic involvement, and the avoidance of unhealthy lifestyle activities was additional common-sense information gleaned from the study. We can hardly ignore the fact that the most common diseases can be prevented or even eliminated with intentional healthy choices.

Pelletier concludes his findings with these words:

> Perhaps the most striking revelation of all in the many hours of talking with the participants in my research study was their abiding commitment to a deeper, altruistic spiritual purpose beyond ourselves. Surely it is the magnitude of what remains to be done for all of humankind that makes genuine humility and compassion so evident in their lives. Now that we are closer than ever to a deeper understanding of mind and body, it seems possible at last to bridge the gap between spiritual purpose and optimal health. Our direction is clear, for medical technology alone cannot provide the answer. Twentieth-century science has permitted humankind to peer with electron microscopes into intercellular space and chart the helical coils of the DNA molecule at the very heart of all life. Arcane Buddhist scriptures formulated thousands of years ago advocated the journey inward toward wisdom and enlightenment, the essence of the soul. Whether we are scientists or mystics, these perennial mysteries instill in us all an abiding sense of awe, humility, and compassion. (1994, p. 276)

In the book *Ageless Body, Timeless Mind,* Deepak Chopra (1993) challenges his reader to discard some assumptions of the old paradigm of health and assume a more enlightened view of existence. He suggests that intelligence can express itself either as thoughts or molecules. An emotion can be described as an abstract feeling or a tangible hormone. In fact, where thoughts go, chemicals go. Thoughts *are* things. Within a year 98 percent of the atoms in the body will have been exchanged for new ones. My question is, will the new atoms be influenced by positive thoughts or negative ones? Chopra suggests that there are three forces pervading all life: creation, maintenance, and destruction. Since humans, unlike other creatures on earth, can change their biology by what they think and feel, humans have the potential to shift the balance of forces toward the creative. These enlightened people grow with full consciousness that they are the source of their own power. Chopra offers seven points that capture the essence of those who shift their lives toward the healthy and the creative.

1. They are able to contact and enjoy silence.
2. They connect with and enjoy Nature.
3. They trust their feelings.
4. They can remain centered and function amid confusion and chaos.
5. They are childlike—they enjoy fantasy and play.
6. They self-refer: They place the highest trust in their own consciousness.
7. They are not rigidly attached to any point of view: Although passionately committed to their creativity, they remain open to new possibilities. (1993, p. 319)

In summary, Chopra suggests that there are infinite ways to acquire creativity and one's true being, but it is love that holds the brightest torch.

Few things reveal the triumphant potential of the human spirit like Victor Frankl's autobiography of his experience in and response to the Nazi concentration camps during World War II. Frankl, a psychiatrist when imprisoned, later became a leader in the field when he introduced logotherapy (spiritual psychotherapy) to the world in the 1950s. His experience at Auschwitz and other death camps captured the most horrific endurance of suffering that one can imagine. He found himself stripped to his naked existence. He witnessed mass deaths, slow starvation, physical and mental violence, cruel diseases, and the removal of all dignity. One thing he did not lose, however, was an inner awareness of his own freedom. Although the Nazi guards, with their cruel hate and predictable prejudices were slaves to their own precepts, Frankl experienced a liberation in the realization that everything can be taken away from a person except one thing: the ability to choose one's attitude in a given set of circumstances. Therein, he grasped how one who has nothing in this world may still know bliss. One's ultimate meaning, he learned, was through transcedent love.

Logos is a Greek word that denotes "meaning." Therefore, logotherapy strives to find meaning in one's life, which according to Frankl is the primary motivational force in humankind. Yet, the word logos also means "spirit" and uniquely dares to enter the spiritual dimension of human existence. For me, Frankl captures the essence of logotherapy with these words of hope:

> By declaring that man is a responsible creature and must actualize the potential meaning of his life, I wish to stress that the true meaning of life is to be found in the world rather than within man or his own *psyche,* as though it were a closed system. By the same token, the real aim of human existence cannot be found in what is called self-actualization. Human existence is essentially self-transcendence rather than self-actualization. Self-actualization is not a possible aim at all, for the simple reason that the more a man would strive for it, the more he would miss it. For only to the extent to which man commits himself to the fulfillment of his life's meaning, to this extent he also actualizes himself. In other words, self-actualization cannot be attained if it is made an end in itself, but only as a side effect of self-transcendence. . . .
>
> A human being is not one thing among others; *things* determine each other, but *man* is ultimately self-determining. What he becomes—within the limits of endowment and environment—he has made out of himself. In the concentration camps, for example, in this living laboratory and on this testing ground, we watched and witnessed some of our comrades behave like swine while others behaved like saints. Man has both potentialities within himself; which one is actualized depends on decisions but not on conditions.

Our generation is realistic, for we have come to know man as he really is. After all, man is that being who has invented the gas chambers of Auschwitz; however, he is also that being who has entered those gas chambers upright, with the Lord's Prayer or the *Shema Yisrael* on his lips. (1977, pp. 212-213)

Even though Frankl later learned that he had also lost his father, mother, brother, and his wife to the ovens of the concentration camps, he continued to give birth to the ultimate meaning of existence and in the process has blessed and given meaning to millions of readers throughout the world.

WELLNESS DEPENDS ON SELF-AWARENESS

To be psychically conflicted is also harmful to wellness. If one does not have a grasp of self, how can he or she be congruent, relate well to others, and set goals? Without intrapersonal awareness and interpersonal skills, how can we accomplish and maintain high-level wellness?

To integrate psychological and spiritual awareness here, one needs to consider only the scriptural commandment that is familiar to most of us, "Thou shalt not bear false witness against thy neighbor" (Exodus 20:16, KJV). It seems to me, with this commandment, we too often settle for a superficial interpretation and miss the true value of the standard presented. We sometimes eat the paper that the menu is written on instead of savoring the feast that the menu is pointing to.

To think that this commandment is only talking about lying is limiting the banquet. We are all witnesses. Not only what we do, but who we are becomes our witness. This commandment doesn't say, "Thou shalt not *tell* false witness." We are not to *bear* false witness against our neighbor.

We need to understand here that everyone we encounter is our neighbor. Even the "bore neigh you" (from where the word originates) is our neighbor. The teaching, herein, is for us to present ourselves to one another honestly. To be pretentious and phony is the personification of bearing false witness.

Before one can avoid bearing false witness, one must first, "Know thyself." If you do not know who you are, how do you know if you are being true to yourself? Perhaps you and I know those who haven't a clue of their incongruence and inconsistency. Indeed, there are those who have not sorted through their psychological makeup, are not concerned about social consistency, and are unaware that their presented thought patterns do not match their desired emotional and behavioral affect. How can they not bear false witness?

This, of course, is not just an individual and personal issue. When we get mixed messages from our government or a beloved organization, this too is confusing. How is it that our country rises up against some atrocities in the world and ignores others? How is it that certain high-ranking military people are ousted for infidelity and others are not? How can we make the removal of the nation's physician-in-chief for condoning masturbation jive with the high ratings of shows such as *Jerry Springer*? How can some talk about love and grace when they promote exclusivity and superiority? Americans are perpetually conflicted.

We perhaps cannot make an immediate impact on the social, political, religious, and medical systems beyond our individuality. I would suggest, however, that we can make a difference in the one arena that this commandment seems to be directed to—in our own lives. Consistency with others is important; congruence with ourselves is essential to health.

ALTERNATIVE AND COMPLEMENTARY FORMS OF WELLNESS

Because of the interconnected nature of optimal health, and the consequent paradigm shift toward wellness, teaching prevention must be primary and the counteractive and suppressive intervention must become secondary. In fact, the word doctor comes from the Latin words for teacher. Andrew Weil, MD, in his best-selling book *Spontaneous Healing,* suggests that conventional medicine seems to have lost sight of this purpose. "We use antispasmodics and antihypertensives, antianxiety agents and antidepressants, antihistamines, antiarrhythmics, antitussives, antipyretics, and antiinflammatories, as well as beta blockers and H_2-receptor antagonists. This is truly antimedicine . . ." (1995, p. 14). In fact, our National Institutes of Health (NIH) have historically focused more on disease than health. We have the National Cancer Institute, the

National Institute of Allergy and Infectious Disease, the National Institute of Arthritis and Skin Diseases, the National Institute of Diabetes and Kidney Disease, and the National Institute of Neurological Disorders and Stroke. Isn't it time for the National Institute for Wellness? In fact, a step in that direction occurred in 1992, when the NIH established the Office of Alternative Medicine with $2 million in federal funds. Funding has periodically increased and in 1999, NIH turned the office into the Center for Complementary and Alternative Medicine, with an allocation of $50 million. The estimated budget for 2003 is $113.2 million (NCCAM, 2002). It clearly seems that with that kind of support, complementary and alternative forms of medical care are here to stay, and the concept of wellness (if not the "Institute") is truly approaching. Indeed a new doctrine is evolving.

Even though complementary and alternative therapies are typically lumped together, there are distinct differences. Alternative is used for those forms of treatment that replace traditional Western medicine, whereas complementary treatment is used along with conventional forms of care. This offers security when treatment modalities such as chiropractic adjustment, biofeedback, hypnotherapy, acupuncture, homeopathy (using highly diluted remedies made from natural substances), and osteopathy (nearly indistinguishable from MDs except for the use of manipulation on all parts of the body) are used as an adjunct to conventional forms of care.

In addition to these forms of complementary care, some others merit alluding to.

Therapeutic touch is a treatment, unlike deep muscle massage or rolfing, where little or no touching occurs. Therapeutic touch is a form of energy healing where energy is transmitted, usually with the therapist's palms, from one part of the body to the part of the patient that is injured or hurting.

Rolfing is a more intense kind of massage and a specific form of bodywork. Rolfing seeks to release repressed emotions as well as dissipate habitual muscle tension. Getting rolfed can be uncomfortable as the therapist applies aggressive pressure on the musculoskeletal system. Afterward, however, most report that the gain was worth the pain.

Biofeedback is a relaxation technique utilizing electronic equipment to amplify and present body responses as they occur. The most basic form is an instrument that measures the external temperature of the hand. More sophisticated forms of biofeedback measure such things as muscle responses and brain waves. As I noted earlier, through biofeedback training I am able to increase or decrease the temperature of my hands with mental effort. Sound mystical? It is not at all. By using certain autogenic phrases, one can see what statement or series of phrases caused biological change. Once these techniques are learned, the equipment may not be necessary to accomplish the change. Biofeedback has been successful in treating migraine headaches, hypertension, bruxism, and other ailments associated with stress as well as seizures and other central nervous system problems.

Hypnosis and the power of suggestion have many ill-founded stereotypes. Most, if not all, of us have experienced hypnosis. In fact, hypnosis is a naturally occurring state where one becomes less aware of the external environment and more aware of the inner world. Hypnotherapy takes advantage of the internal connectedness of the person and uses verbal suggestions to accomplish extraordinary states of awareness and impressive physiological changes. Hypnosis is not projected on the patient, it is not a sleep experience, and it is not a dangerous exercise. Generally speaking, hypnosis is a focused form of inner attention, which allows the patient's unconscious mind to search for new alternatives, new skills, new coping strategies, and new potentials. Some dentists use hypnosis for comfort and pain control. Women have given birth while under hypnosis. Surgeries have been accomplished with hypnosis being the only form of anesthesia. Some other common uses for hypnosis are weight control, smoking cessation, skin rashes, gastrointestinal problems, allergies, pain control, and anxiety.

Dr. James Braid, a Scottish surgeon, introduced the term hypnotism in 1843. Braid expanded his knowledge from the work done by Franz Anton Mesmer in the eighteenth century. Mesmer's work was at the least controversial, yet his name has passed into the language as both a noun and a verb (mesmerism and mesmerize). Braid, in understanding that the process produced what he recognized to be a "nervous sleep" (due to the rapid eye movement), called the experience hypnosis. As it has turned out, another label would have been more fitting. Hypnosis got its name from Hypnos, the Greek god of sleep. His brother Thanatos, the god of death, would appear to have a great deal in common. That is, a sleeping person may appear to be dead and a dead person may appear to be sleeping. This is the problem with the term hypnosis because the experience is not a sleep experience. In fact, the term "hyper-alert" may better capture the experience because one's senses are more keen while under hypnosis. This notwithstanding, the label of hypnosis seems here to stay, and hypnosis is a marvelous tool to aid in wellness.

Expectation is a definite ingredient in our paradigm of health. A few years ago I was building a deck on the back of my house and noticed my little finger bleeding profusely. I do not know how or exactly when the cut occurred. I do know that it did not hurt until I noticed it. Once I did notice it and realized that it should hurt, indeed it did. This reveals not only the perception component of pain and the course one expects it to take, but also the broader scope of illness and unconscious honoring of individual expectations.

Only a few years ago certain surgeries, performed quite similarly today, required periods of bed rest and hospital stays that would be considered excessive today. Certainly, in some cases, procedures are different and surgical wounds are smaller. Yet, if one accepts the programming that he or she will not be able to get out of bed for five days, that suggestion or belief system carries the authoritative response.

When I was in Vietnam, my unit's mamasan went home one evening, had a baby, and was back working at 7:30 a.m. the next morning. When I asked her how she was able to do this, it was my question that seemed strange and not her indefatigability. When my first child was born natural childbirth was feared—today it is practiced, albeit not with the same resolve as that possessed by that mamasan some thirty years ago.

Prayer is an exercise that need not be only associated with a worship service. Most everyone has offered some kind of a prayer at some point in his or her life. Many people pray at least on a daily basis. The point here, as has been stated earlier, is that there is a growing base of research that supports the beneficial effects of prayer on health.

Engaging in positive beliefs, realizing the oneness of our nature, and desiring wholeness seems to resonate with all we can say about wellness. Still, some research shows prayer to be effective even when sick people are unaware that they are the objects of prayer. Most religions have a model prayer which tends to be comprehensive in nature and purposeful to that tradition.

Nutrition not only nourishes the body, when proper and balanced, but it also promotes growth and healing. Most of us accept the fact that what we take into our bodies makes a difference with our health. Certainly illegal drugs are not healthy. Likewise, prescription drugs are harmful if not taken as prescribed and are sometimes harmful even if taken as prescribed. We know that good nutrition is crucial to good health, yet we sometimes still practice unhealthy eating habits. I do not wish here to include a comprehensive summary of healthy eating. What I would like to include are some nutritional points that have been advocated by dietary experts for years. Most of what I say will likely be familiar. Much is common sense, yet I expect that some of the information will be both new and helpful.

As we seek to make healthy choices in our lives, what we eat is particularly important because this is a choice we make several times a day. The old computer phrase, "Garbage in, garbage out," comes to mind.

A comedian once said, "If I would have known how long I was going to live, I would have taken better care of myself." Well, perhaps we can start this journey of healthy eating now. It is reasonable to accept that healthy eating promotes a healthy life.

It is not surprising that U.S. citizens eat too much. When I was a child, a great portion of our food was raised on our property in Missouri. Food came not only from our vegetable garden but also from our chicken house and pig lot. Special foods such as oranges and nuts were enjoyed only at Christmas time. What is now commonplace seafood was unheard of for my family. Now the supermarket has virtually any food—anytime. We are tempted with commercials and advertising urging us to eat this and try that. A mere sampling of the vast variety would be overwhelming. The meta-communication of this advertising allows one to believe that the food being advertised might make the consumer more physically fit, less depressed, and perhaps even sexy. If the food leaves you with heartburn, then there is a quick fix for that, too. Fast food is not only the theme of some drive-through distributors of food that is perhaps less than nutritious, it is a lifestyle which has become too common in the United States.

My point is that we can improve our nutritional intake by not only eating less (in some cases much less), but we can also experience greater wellness if we become more selective in what we eat.

An initial step in the direction of health is to reduce the intake of all types of fat, especially those derived from animals. Nutritional research categorically reveals that reducing fat intake not only helps in keeping body weight at healthy levels, but it also helps to prevent many serious illnesses. It is possible to maintain healthy levels of protein without all the meat that the average American consumes. Fish, poultry, and certain vegetables (such as tofu and beans) are great substitutes for red meat.

High levels of saturated fat stimulate the liver to make more LDL (bad) cholesterol than the body can eliminate. This results in damage to arterial walls, a gradual compromising of the cardiovascular system, and, ultimately, disabling heart disease.

Frying food with animal fat is not only unhealthy, it is unnecessary. Olive oil is regarded the "best and safest of all edible fats" (Weil, 1995, p. 142). To remove the polyunsaturated vegetable oils, margarines, and the other forms of animal fat from the kitchen and replace them with olive oil is to make giant strides in the direction of wellness.

Fatty red meats should be replaced by fish with omega-3 fatty acids (such as salmon, sardines, mackerel, and herring). Omega-3 fatty acids are believed to reduce inflammatory changes in the body, and perhaps protect against cancer. These omega-3 fatty acids can also be purchased in capsules of fish oil at health food stores.

Other healthy eating habits include eating complex carbohydrates (whole grains, beans, fresh fruits, and vegetables). People should eat at least three helpings of fresh fruit and five helpings of uncooked or steamed vegetables every day.

Most everyone has heard this before, but human beings need at least eight, eight-ounce glasses of water each day. This helps in keeping the body hydrated so that the necessary elimination processes are optimal.

Supplements are dietary additives intended to make up for any deficiencies in the body's systems. If the body is operating efficiently as it is intended, and dietary intake is healthy, then the systems convert the food into necessary substances and energy to maintain optimal health. However, the human system is always dynamic, ever changing, and (hopefully) never static. Consequently, homeostasis is a process. When the body is under stress for instance, the mental activities may not be positive, the proper chemistry may be disrupted, and the immune system may be compromised. Anyone dealing with a disease or who is prone to illness should investigate whether certain dietary (or vitamin and mineral) supplements may be indicated. People should check with their medical doctor (who is hopefully holistic) to see what is right for them. Also, there is a wealth of information on this subject in countless books. Everyone needs to educate themselves.

Having said this, there is one suggestion that I would make: take antioxidants to guard against free radicals. Oxidation is a corrosive force in nature, which can rust cars, damage the ozonosphere, and cause cancer. Consuming fresh fruits and vegetables is a very important preventive measure. Yet it is safe and effective to also take vitamin C, vitamin E, selenium, and beta-carotene in tablet form.

Physical exercise is integral to health. Exercise keeps the systems of the body operating efficiently so that each system may interface with the others and accomplish optimal health. Those who exercise regularly know that physical exercise doesn't require as much energy as it generates. Many people report that regular exercise makes them feel younger, more energetic, and more alive. Those who exercise on a consistent basis tend to sleep better, relax more easily, and are even more attentive to healthier eating habits.

During the summer of 1999, when the bulk of this manuscript was written, I found that the replacement of my exercise program with my writing project could only last a few weeks before I experienced the waning of my energy and creativity. Within days of resuming my exercise program, I was back where I needed to be and equipped with a valuable lesson: I cannot trade my exercise program for anything for very long. Just as one cannot obtain health in an external and uninvolved way, one cannot acquire the benefits of exercise without engaging in the experience of exercise.

For physical exercise to be well rounded, aerobic exercise for the cardiovascular system, strength building for muscles and bones, and stretching for flexibility are all needed.

Aerobic exercise is activity that increases heart rate, breathing, and perspiration. The appropriate level of exertion depends on age and level of physical fitness. Certainly the beginner must consult his or her physician or a qualified physical instructor. Activities such as jogging, fast walking, biking, rowing, and active swimming are aerobic.

Building up, over time, to rigorous exercise three or four times per week for about thirty minutes each session seems to be sufficient for optimal results. The benefits of aerobic exercise for the cardiovascular system are hardly disputed. It stimulates the heart and lungs in becoming more efficient in oxygen flow and blood gas exchanges. It also helps in the overall elimination processes of the body as well as stimulates the release of endorphins in the brain that improve mood and enhance energy.

The benefits of weight-resistance exercise are also significant. Strengthened and toned muscles are an added reserve against sprains, strains, or even breaks. This firmer foundation builds confidence, adds endurance, and even fosters self-esteem. Lifting weights and doing calisthenics are forms of strengthening exercises, and almost every local health club is equipped with a variety of weight-lifting equipment.

All physical activity must begin and end with stretching exercises. Again, a physician or exercise instructor can demonstrate various stretching exercises that will give attention to all major muscle groups. Stretching promotes flexibility that enhances posture, improves joints, and actually strengthens muscles.

As the body becomes better tuned and more efficient, it is only reasonable to expect that the various systems of the body will be more capable of accomplishing the individual tasks achieving the unified goal of wellness.

Personally, I exercise about five times per week. I begin with about ten minutes of stretching and then move to the weight lifting part of the health club where I go through a routine of various machines that address all major muscle groups. Amazingly, I can move through this portion of my program in about fifteen minutes. I then run for about thirty minutes where I elevate my heart rate from about 65 beats per minute (at rest) to about 130-140 per minute while doing my aerobic exercise. I occasionally engage in energy bursts, which elevate my heart rate even more, but always stay within my determined limits. It would be unwise for anyone to start an exercise program and seek to raise the heart rate by double. Age, fitness, and overall health must be considered in determining how to begin and then accelerate an exercise program.

There is a form of exercise that many consider to be safe, ultimately beneficial, and relatively risk free: walking. For most of us, it is something we have been doing for years, yet not to the extent that we can, or perhaps need to. If the walking is brisk, it is aerobic; if it is leisurely, it is still beneficial.

Most people in the world walk much more than the average American. Many walk out of necessity, some for practicality, some for leisure. I was in Germany in the spring of 1999 and was impressed not only by the number of people who walked, but also by how walking is incorporated into the social and community structure. I was struck that the small villages of Bavaria were not only connected with roads for the motor vehicles, but many were also connected by exquisite walkways occupied by pedestrians.

Andrew Weil, one of the world's leading physicians in the field of health and wellness, says that "walking is the most healthful form of physical activity, the one that has the greatest capacity to keep the healing system in good working order and increases the likelihood of spontaneous healing in case of illness" (1995, p. 189). Indeed, we are made to walk.

Relaxation fully occurs when the total self (mind, body, and spirit) is at rest—calm and peaceful. Trying to be relaxed and well without sufficient sleep is not possible. The average person requires about eight hours of sleep per night (or per day), but an occasional power nap can work wonders for those who are sleep deprived.

There are additional ways to obtain optimal relaxation. One way to enhance relaxation is to utilize a simple breathing technique. While sitting or lying down, take in a long, deep breath using the diaphragm to inflate the lungs. Slowly exhale through pursed lips until all the air is gone. Now quickly move again to a slow inhalation. As you continue to do this, think of inhaling calm and comfort and think of exhaling tension and discomfort. Repeat the process twelve times. The deep breathing may cause feelings of light-headedness. That is why it is necessary to be sitting or lying down. The exercise may also cause the need to yawn. Go ahead and yawn, but do not count the quick inhalation of a yawn as one of the twelve deep breaths and slow exhalations. After the exercise, assess how you feel relative to when you began. Indeed, it is a meaningful technique for relaxation. Do this at least once a day.

I would now like to offer a more inclusive and structured relaxation exercise. By all means, sit or lie down. If you choose to sit, sit back in a chair with your back straight and your feet flat on the floor. Allow your hands to lay palms up in your lap. These instructions will assume a sitting posture, yet you can accommodate these instructions while lying on your back. You may acquaint yourself with the flow of information in this exercise, or better, have someone read the sequence in a soft voice, pausing briefly after each suggestion to relax. At first take ten to fifteen minutes for this exercise. After a few times, take about thirty minutes for the experience.

Begin by taking a slow and deep breath using your diaphragm to inflate your lungs. As you slowly exhale, say to yourself, "I will become very relaxed." Now close your eyes and take a second breath. As you exhale, say to yourself, "I will become very relaxed." With both hands make fists and notice the tension. Relax your hands after about five seconds and notice the contrast between the tension you created and the calm in your hands that you now feel. Now bend your arms at the elbows and flex your bicep muscles. After about five seconds, relax and lower your arms back to your lap. Now point both arms out from you, making them rigid and flexing your tricep muscles. After about five seconds, relax and appreciate the contrast as your arms lay heavy on your lap. At this time, shrug your shoulders by pulling them up toward your ears. Hold that pose for about five seconds and again relax. Notice the heaviness of your arms as they lay on your lap. Think of the effort it would require to lift your arms, but you do not have to—you are reposed and calm. Now tilt your head forward leaning your chin toward your chest. Lean your head to the left touching your left shoulder with your left ear. Do the same thing in the other direction, touching your right shoulder with your right ear. Follow that by tilting your head backward—not so far that it hurts—just far enough to flex your neck muscles and notice the tension. Now allow your head to be centrally balanced and slightly forward and experience the relaxation. Say to yourself, "I am becoming relaxed." As you continue with your eyes closed, raise your eyebrows, causing horizontal wrinkles across your forehead. Turn the horizontal wrinkles into vertical ones by creating a frown. Relax, allowing your forehead to smooth. Gently squeeze your eyes together. You are squeezing out the tension. Enjoy the calm and peace as you release the tension from your eyes and relax. Now snarl your nose, make a snooty expression, and sense the tension involved in this movement. Now, again, contrast the relaxation. Gently bite your teeth together, paying attention to the tautness in your jaw. Relax. Press your tongue against the roof of your mouth and notice the tension in your throat. Relax. Now begin to notice the looseness and calm throughout your face, scalp, and entire head. Say to yourself, "I am calm and quiet. I am comfortable and content. I am becoming very relaxed . . . I am at peace. . . ."

Now without significantly altering your posture, arch your back away from the back of the chair. Detect the flexed muscles in your back. Again, relax. Now pull your stomach in, flexing your abdominal muscles. Enjoy the contrast as you relax. At this time take another slow breath, inhaling comfort and peace and exhaling discomfort and tension. Breathe deeply again pulling in the healing energy from the universe and releasing any bad thoughts and feelings when you exhale. Repeat these breaths two more times. Now the entire upper portion of your body is relaxed. Notice for the first time the heaviness of your arms as they lay on your lap. Consider for an instant what it would take to lift your arms—you do not have to. The relaxation desires to spread. Say to yourself, "I am relaxed. . . ." As you continue, flex your buttock muscles, discern the muscles, and now release the forces of exertion. Now raise your legs until they are straight out from the chair and your knees are locked. Recognize the tautness in your thigh muscles. Relax, with your feet again flat on the floor. With your toes on the floor, raise your heels up and flex your calf muscles. Relax with your feet back on the floor. With your heels on the floor, raise the front of your feet and flex your shin muscles. Relax and contrast the difference between the tension and the relaxation. Say to yourself, "I am very relaxed, I am comfortable and quiet." Notice now your heaviness in the chair—how the chair is supporting you in your effortless relaxation.

Now, take five slow and comfortable breaths and, as you do, identify any tension that may still reside anywhere. If tension is sensed, allow the forces of gravity to pull this remnant tension down to your feet. On your fifth deep breath, picture a small valve opening on the bottom of each foot, allowing the remaining tension to flow out. As the valves close, they seal your entire system with pure relaxation and peace of mind. Allow only a contented smile and sentiment of gratitude as your entire being bathes in peace.

Now we are going to increase this sense of harmony and health as you picture a shaft of light covering your whole being. You alone give this light meaning. Perhaps it is the healing energy of the universe;

perhaps it is the loving energy of the Divine. Regardless of the inter-pretation, you are penetrated with wholeness. Now, slowly count from one to five, slowly opening your eyes on the count of five. Take a deep breath and take this relaxation with you.

A relaxed body lends to efficiently operating glands and organs. An efficient system is a healthy system.

PRACTICING HOLISTIC WELLNESS

Following are a few suggestions for the enhancement of wellness. The ideas are separated into the three categories of body, mind, and spirit, and one other category of healthy concepts. As I have explained before, I do not think one can in reality separate these dimensions. The mind is the body and the spirit is the mind. Therefore, what is listed under the heading "body," may just as well be listed under one of the other headings and vice versa. I do not *have* a body, I *am* my body. It is not that I *have* a spirit, I *am* spirit. Indeed, to exercise my body accomplishes the enhancement of my mind, the improvement of my intellect, and the strengthening of my emotions. Exercise, of course, is also good for the body. Having said this, hopefully these suggestions will prove helpful. This is far from a comprehensive list of activities for optimal health, but I trust it will provide an appropriate sampling.

Body

1. Get to know your medical doctor and allow your doctor to get to know you. Schedule appropriate periodic physical exams.
2. Understand the value of alternative or complementary forms of medical care such as acupuncture, biofeedback, chiropractic, homeopathy, and osteopathy.
3. Practice good nutrition and herbal therapy by eating a balanced diet with vegetables, fruits, and grains and cutting back on or eliminating such things as junk food, animal fat, salt, caffeine, alcohol, nicotine, and other harmful drugs.
4. Drink eight glasses of water per day. (A six-pack of beer is not a substitute.)

5. Take vitamin supplements as may be indicated—especially antioxidants.
6. Engage in a consistent exercise program of aerobics, weight lifting, stretching, and walking.
7. Take advantage of such experiences as massage therapy, therapeutic touch, and hugging.
8. Know your cholesterol levels and resolve to keep the levels within the accepted range.
9. Get enough sleep to experience full mind, body, and spirit renewal (usually about eight hours per night).
10. List the behaviors or activities that you consider harmful to your health and replace them with healthier alternatives.

Mind

1. Practice meditation and relaxation to reduce stress and become centered through such techniques as transcendental meditation, deep muscle relaxation, self-hypnosis, breathing exercises, or yoga.
2. Stimulate the senses with tranquility and beauty, utilizing aroma therapy, listening to therapeutic music, and taking long nature walks.
3. Picture yourself healthy and full of energy.
4. Resolve to maintain a positive or optimistic mental attitude.
5. Seek every day to improve your congruence with yourself and consistency with others.
6. Care for your mind by learning new left-brain activities that are analytical, rational, or verbal, and new right-brain activities that are artistic, intuitive, and playful.
7. Seek to tell, hear, or read one humorous story every day and smile more.
8. Acquire a personal psychotherapist.
9. Set personal goals and evaluate them regularly.
10. Quickly identify attitudes and emotions that are counterproductive to well-being (such as hate, guilt, fear, prejudice, and dependency) and seek to better manage them.

Spirit

1. Consider that spiritual health is at the heart of wholeness and intentionally nurture your spiritual dimension.
2. Desire for your spiritual or religious beliefs to foster love, hope, trust, self-esteem, forgiveness, and responsibility.
3. Commit to love and accept yourself.
4. Contemplate that the essence of your being is love.
5. Nurture your spirit of altruism and concern for others.
6. Be philanthropic and give of your time, talents, and resources to a worthy cause.
7. Practice prayer and positive intentionality.
8. Learn to be one with nature, assuming responsibility for environmental care.
9. Acquire the services of a spiritual director.
10. Resist gestures of power, supremacy, and prejudice and seek forgiveness, value clarification, and congruence.

Other Wellness Concepts

1. Wear your seat belt or cycling helmet.
2. Listen to the subtle messages of the mind, body, and spirit, such as, "slow down," "relax," or "trust."
3. Take several minivacations or some change of pace throughout the year.
4. Affirm or compliment members of your immediate family and someone beyond your family every day.
5. Determine one thing you could do today that would improve a suffering relationship.
6. Implement one thing this week that would improve your work.
7. Vegetating is not relaxing and being a couch potato is not taking care of yourself.
8. Grow and maintain a garden of vegetables and/or flowers.
9. Do all that you do in moderation.
10. Obtaining help is a sign of strength.
11. Do to others as you would that they do to you (the Golden Rule).
12. Remember, your greatest doctor is the one within.

INCENTIVES FOR WELLNESS

Sociologists hold that even though individuals possess free will, we are all influenced by social and cultural factors. Certainly we must individually be responsible for taking care of ourselves. We must practice wellness. Yet, companies can seek to create a culture for the enhancement of health. Creativity may be the modus operandi for producing an environment for healthy lifestyles and healthy living. Here is a beginning list of incentives that you may introduce in your workplace. Modify and add to the list periodically.

1. Install television monitors in the company cafeteria that provide information on such things as healthy eating, risky drinking, community resources, and rewards and incentives for participants in your company's wellness program.
2. Free, healthy lunch when attending company-related workshops (such as stress management, conflict resolution, family harmony, addictions, wellness issues) during lunchtime.
3. Free health club membership for former smokers, if tobacco-free for one year.
4. A monetary award per cholesterol point reduced from one heath fair to the next.
5. Prize to the winner of a "Best Healthy Menu" contest.
6. Cash award for walking/running a certain number of miles (twenty-five miles per month, fifty miles per month).
7. Prize to the winner of a "Laughter is Good Medicine" contest.
8. Nominations for and prize to the winner of "Kindest Gesture of the Month" contest.
9. Hot wax hand treatment for arthritic hands.
10. Develop a system to utilize a massage therapist on a periodic basis.

Conclusion

We are interconnected. We are connected by the many dimensions that make up the human entity. We are connected with the greater community of humanity. Thus, our health is equally interconnected. The quality of this interconnectedness parallels the quality of our health.

The concept of the psyche as mind is embraced by many people. Intelligence as well as cognitive and emotional processes are a part of our psyche. Psyche as the seat of the human soul is an understanding that is not so prevalent. Even so, the human spirit, self-awareness, personal congruence, values, and integrity are also part of our psyche. Anyone who thinks that the psyche does not affect the soma (body) must think again. Psychergonomics not only embraces this awareness but also points to how this interconnectedness affects our health and well-being. A change in the status of one part of a person changes the collective status of that person. Indeed, we are awesomely and "wonderfully made" (Psalm 139:14 KJV).

Many health care professionals are prepared to integrate mental and spiritual health with physical wellness to achieve human wholeness. Yet I state again that the certified profession chaplains or the credentialed pastoral counselors who have advanced degrees in both mental health and theology are eminently prepared to promote the concept of psychergonomics in the workplace.

The most important ingredient for the accomplishment of your wellness, however, is you. Ultimately we all must take charge of and responsibility for our own wellness. No one plays a bigger part in your wellness than you do. So as you nurture your spirit, enhance your mind, and take care of your body, may your wholeness be accomplished.

Appendix

Understanding for Wellness

This appendix of *Psychergonomics* provides a sampling of troubling issues common in our society. Ultimate answers to these problems are not provided. I do not believe that the ultimate answers exist. Instead, in summary fashion, information is offered to further equip the reader with helpful information.

Someone once said, "Ignorance is bliss." I leave with you, "Understanding is healthy."

UNDERSTANDING ADDICTIONS

When one considers the subject of addictions, drugs or alcohol usually come to mind. The stark reality is, however, that there are numerous substances, activities, and processes that may be addictive to anyone prone to addictive behaviors. Underlying all addictions are unconscious dynamics and processes which, when linked with existing genetic and biological factors, facilitate cravings and addictions.

In fact, it is more meaningful to talk about the underlying addictive dynamics than it is to differentiate between a compulsive gambler and a sex addict. Fundamentally at work within the life of an addicted personality are excessive and abnormal pursuits of control (over their world and other people), emotional highs (which includes different or new sensations and thrills), and security (which may be a primordial attempt to be in the womb again).

To ignore these underlying issues may allow a recovering alcoholic to become a shopping or spending addict or perhaps a workaholic. All addictions have an appealing side to them—that's why they are pursued. Yet, fundamentally, addictions are progressively destructive.

No one is certain how much of a role genetics plays in a given addiction, yet most professionals believe that heredity is a part of the formula. Other factors such as lifestyle and personality traits are also to be considered. Psychological issues such as a fragile ego, a tendency toward unrealistic thinking, and a strong need for excitement and stimulation may be precursors for developing an addiction.

Not long ago it was believed that addiction had to create a crisis in order for changes to occur. However, tough-love types of intervention coupled with therapy and education are proving very successful.

Addiction Is a Disease

The American Medical Association has recognized addiction as a disease since 1956 (Haynes, 1988).

Left untreated, alcoholism and other drug addictions are as chronic and terminal as cancer, diabetes, and heart disease (Alters, 2002).

Substances That May Become Addictive

- Alcohol
- Prescription drugs
- Over-the-counter drugs
- Illegal drugs
- Tobacco
- Inhalants
- Adrenaline rush

Interventions that have proven to work the best for most are twelve-step programs such as Gamblers Anonymous, Narcotics Anonymous, Alcoholics Anonymous, and Debtors Anonymous.

Activities That May Become Addictive

- Eating
- Spending
- Gambling
- Exercise
- Work
- Sex
- Romance
- Computer
- Religion
- Codependency

Signs of Addiction

- Preoccupation with X (the addictive substance or activity)
- Inability to resist, control, or stop X
- Increased tension prior to X
- Frequent and progressive involvement with X
- Inordinate amount of time spent on X
- Progressive deception and dishonesty regarding involvement with X
- Engaging in X to the neglect of job, school, family, and social obligations
- Pleasure while experiencing X
- Continuation of X in spite of problems posed

A computer can be to the computer addict what shopping can be to the spending addict, what the lottery ticket can be to the gambling addict, what the syringe can be to the heroin addict, what the valium can be to the prescription drug addict, what the bottle can be to the alcoholic. . . .

Help Is Available

Depending on the addiction and on the individual's unique pyscho-social-biological profile, certain psychotropic medications, including anti-depressants, may be indicated. Psychotherapy and treatment by an addictions specialist are beneficial in most cases. Support groups, especially ones that incorporate a twelve-step model, are particularly helpful.

UNDERSTANDING ALCOHOLISM

In 1990, the American Society of Addiction Medicine and the National Council on Alcoholism and Drug Dependence adopted this definition of alcoholism:

Alcoholism is a primary, chronic disease with genetic, psychological, and environmental factors influencing its development and manifestations. The disease is often progressive and fatal. It is characterized by continuous or periodic:

- impaired control over drinking
- preoccupation with the drug alcohol
- use of alcohol despite adverse consequences
- distortions in thinking, most notably denial (Klier, Quiram, and Siegel, 1999)

If one's drinking causes problems (social, legal, financial, marital, employment) and one continues to drink—he or she is probably an alcoholic.

An Alcoholic Cannot Not Drink

Myth:

- Alcoholism only happens to emotionally troubled or morally weak people.
- If one only drinks beer, he or she will not become an alcoholic.
- One has to drink every day to be an alcoholic.
- One will not become an alcoholic if one can "hold his or her liquor."
- "Alcoholism can never happen to me."
- "I am not hurting anyone but myself."

Fact:

- Anyone can become addicted to alcohol.
- Most emotional problems associated with alcoholism are the result of the disease and not its cause.
- How much and how often one drinks is a more important issue than why one drinks or the personality one possesses.
- It's not the kind of person that is the issue; it is the kind of drinking.
- Alcoholism is more frequent in groups that accept heavy drinking or drunkenness and in groups whose members get mixed messages about alcohol.
- Alcoholism runs in families. Children who have a biological parent with alcoholism are four times more likely to develop alcoholism than those whose parents did not have alcoholism.
- Kids will do what parents do and not what parents say.

Everyone has some level of biological risk for alcoholism. One can choose to drink or choose not to drink but cannot choose his or her body's reaction to drinking.

About 6.6 percent of the American workforce reports heavy drinking (i.e., five or more drinks per day on five or more days in the past thirty days) (NIDA, 1999).

The cost of alcoholism and related problems to the United States is an estimated $185 billion per year (NIAAA, 2001).

What Is a Drink?

- One 12-ounce beer at 4 percent alcohol
- One 4-ounce glass of wine at 12 percent alcohol
- One 1-ounce shot glass of liquor at 50 percent alcohol (100 proof)

These various forms of alcohol may affect people in different ways, depending on how one's body metabolizes the alcohol. Factors such as body size, age, sex, rate of consumption, health status, fatigue level, altitude, stomach contents, and the use of other drugs affect how the body may react to alcohol.

Risks of Alcohol Consumption

- One to two drinks per day
  —No known risk
- Three drinks per day
  —Increase in blood pressure
  —Increase in heart disease
  —Increase in cirrhosis of the liver
- Four drinks per day
  —Increased risk of impairment problems
- Five drinks per day
  —Increased social problems
  —Shortened life span
- Six or more drinks per day
  —Increased problems associated with alcoholism (Daugherty and O'Bryan, 1990)

Impairment While Driving Under the Influence of Alcohol

Blood Alcohol Level (BAL)	.02	.08	.10	.15
Risk of automobile accidents	None	3 times	4 times	8 times
Driving status	Sober	DUI	Intoxicated	Intoxicated
Minimum wait before driving home	None	1 hr.	3 hrs.	6 hrs.

(Adapted from Daugherty and O'Bryan, 1990, p. 12)

UNDERSTANDING ANGER

Contrary to popular belief, anger is not a choice. One does not choose to get angry, but one can choose what he or she will do with the anger when it is present. Anger is our body's response to injustices and threats. With this awareness, anger can be a redeeming motivator to make things better in our world. In this regard, it is unfortunate if one does nothing and denies his or her feelings. In fact, it can be as destructive to do nothing with your anger as it is to lash out at others with your anger. If you do nothing with your anger, you violate the purpose of the emotion. How can you correct an injustice or remove a threat if you do nothing? In addition, to do nothing causes depression which is unhealthy to the self, or anger may slip out in the form of passive aggression which is hurtful to others. Anger, like all emotions, must be managed and controlled. When acknowledged and managed, anger is redeeming to the world in that we are seeking to make things better and less threatening. When anger is uncontrolled or out of control, threatening situations increase instead of being reduced.

There are two helpful ways of looking at anger. One is linear. That is, on a scale of 1 to 10, how intense is my anger?

Another model of understanding anger is to compare it to an egg. Herein, the surface or shell is the *observed anger,* the egg white represents the *threat,* and it all surrounds the yolk and protects the *hurt.* At anger's core is hurt.

With this awareness, when one says, "I was not angry, I was frustrated," he or she is saying that the feeling could be more intense, but it needs to be acknowledged that the feeling is anger. When one says, "I was more hurt than angry," he or she is going to the core of the issue, yet still needs to acknowledge the presence of anger.

This awareness illuminates the concept of holism. People do not leave their emotions at the plant or office door whether they are coming or going. To realize that emotions have an impact on how people function is a meaningful understanding. Everyone from the manager to the assembly person hired yesterday, from the teacher to the student can be on top of the world or somewhat under par and the reasons will be multidimensional—even emotional. To have resources to assist with a bombarded ego, relational strife, emotional stress, difficult children, aging and dependent parents, financial problems, a health crisis, and an infinite array of troubling situations is as beneficial to a company as an alcohol treatment program is.

The statement "Leave your personal problems at the door" is like saying "Don't think of pink elephants."

No Problems Allowed

Anger is an energy producing emotion! When people get angry, the energy may hurt by:

- Generating too much adrenaline and other chemicals
- Causing the heart to pound
- Increasing blood pressure
- Tensing muscles
- Making them shake
- Creating digestive problems
- Causing a headache

- Increasing proneness to accidents
- Causing them to lash out physically or emotionally

When people get angry, the energy may help motivate them to:

- Defend their rights
- Protect their freedom
- Explore and understand their feelings
- Accomplish their goals
- Develop an appreciation of others' uniqueness and strengthen relationships
- Enhance communications
- Teach patience
- Create growth

Ways to Manage Anger

Do Not Ignore It

The most corrosive thing that people can do with anger is nothing. To do nothing is a violation of the emotion's purpose. There are many ways that ignoring anger will backfire. All are destructive. Instead, people need to respond to anger in productive and healthy ways.

Share Concerns

Confiding in someone trustworthy (friend, spouse, pastor, doctor, or counselor) is beneficial. Just talking can help. The processing of thoughts and feelings is therapeutic, and the feedback can be enlightening.

Physical Exercise

Any kind of aerobic exercise burns off adrenaline and other chemicals that anger produces. People should consult their physician to determine what exercise program is right for them.

Rest and Relax

Engage in meaningful and restful activities. Read a book, watch a movie, go for a hike, go golfing, go fishing, do needlework, work in the garden, resurrect an old hobby, do relaxation and breathing exercises. Be sure to get enough sleep.

Prayer and Meditation

Taking individual needs and limitations to an external power is therapeutic. Awareness of being accepted and loved is very comforting.

UNDERSTANDING CONFLICTS

Conflicts are internal and external. A dilemma of choice occurs when a person must select one of two undesirable alternatives. It may be less stressful to have to choose one of two desirable activities, yet the choice still presents a motivational conflict. Internal conflicts also result from unconscious behavior and beliefs that are incongruent, or at odds with one's values and conscious goals. These kinds of conflicts drain energy and often cause people to be moody.

Most often, however, conflicts are considered in an external and relational context. Conflicts occur in marriages, families, among friends, at work, and even between strangers, as road rage reveals. Yet the best way to minimize interpersonal conflicts is to resolve any internal conflicts that may be sabotaging personal actions.

Other causes of interpersonal conflict include competition for resources, the desire for revenge, selfish and egocentric gestures, and faulty communication practices.

Points of Understanding

- Conflict is more common than we acknowledge.
- Perceived attacks usually are not meant to be as personal as they feel.
- Accepting appropriate responsibility for the conflict is important.
- Conflicts usually are not linear; rather, they involve multiple or circular causality.
- Conflicts usually result from unresolved issues of the past.
- Confrontation may be a form of caring.
- If people act before they talk, then they are starting backward.
- It is essential to be persistent in attempts for resolution.
- Be assertive in communicating needs.
- Offer positive feedback rather than negative criticism.
- Consult someone with a neutral perspective.
- Peace comes when we accept that we cannot change other people.

Most professionals who are involved in conflict resolution report that conflict resolution has a healthy dimension. That is, if the energy from a conflict is managed as opposed to being squelched or ignored, the result may be beneficial for all involved. If the best of all sides of an issue is presented and heard, the creativity of the process may result in a win-win scenario at a higher level than could have been achieved otherwise.

Did you know that no one can make you feel a certain way? We are responsible for our own feelings, reactions, and behaviors.

Unmanaged Conflict

- Increases stress
- Creates hidden agendas
- Causes defensiveness
- Stifles creativity
- Wastes energy, time, and resources
- Promotes illness
- Harms relationships

Just as nothing breeds success like success, nothing breeds conflict like conflict.

Managed Conflict

- Encourages communication
- Is focused and orderly
- Recognizes strength in diversity
- Experiences disagreement without personal attacks
- Harnesses creativity
- Seeks win-win resolution
- Promotes wholeness and wellness

The greatest ingredient to conflict resolution, and indeed to good mental health, is empathy. The greatest obstacle is the inability to forgive.

A Personal Exercise

1. An internal conflict which I have yet to resolve is . . .
2. The best way for me to resolve this internal conflict is to . . .
3. My greatest interpersonal conflict seems to be with . . .
4. I know that the relationship with whom I have a conflict can improve if I would . . .
5. Some of the things this conflict has taught me are . . .

Ways to Cope

- Utilize safe and healthy ways to blow off steam.
- Access support systems.
- Identify and understand feelings.
- Release fantasies of retribution.
- Picture being in harmony with others.
- Practice relaxation and meditation.
- Seek professional help before conflict drains your energy.

UNDERSTANDING DEPRESSION

Whereas anger is accompanied by energy—positive and negative—depression is accompanied by lethargy. Depression may be a symptom. That is, it may be a signal that something is out of balance physically, emotionally, or spiritually. Moreover, depression may be a disease in and of itself, threatening well-being on many fronts. A depressed person may have mild mood changes and say, "I feel down in the dumps," or feel dangerously hopeless and say, "I wish I were dead."

Probably the most frequent complaint bringing people to psychotherapists', ministers', and physicians' offices is the pain of depression. Depression affects one's emotions and spirit but also attacks one's physical well-being with potentially drastic results. At some time and to some degree most everyone will experience depression.

Depression as a symptom (referred to as exogenous) results from losses. The losses may be concrete such as a death, a divorce, or the loss of a prized possession. The losses may be abstract such as the loss of love, respect, authority, or status. The losses may be potential such as a lump in the breast, a dreaded diagnosis, or the threat of losing employment. Depression also results from internalizing (as opposed to appropriately expressing) certain emotions such as anger, guilt, or fear.

In severe cases, depression is clinical and biological (referred to as endogenis). This includes such illnesses as major clinical depression, bipolar disorder (manic depression), and seasonal affective disorder (SAD). Depression is like a fever in that something causes it. It must be pointed out, however, that there does not seem to be any demonstrated differences in symptomology if its source is internal and biological (endogenous) or external and situational (exogenous). Some believe that mood can affect body chemistry and body chemistry can affect mood.

Myths About Depression

MYTH: Clinical depression is a character flaw or a sign of weakness.

FACT: No one, regardless of his or her status in life, is exempt from the potential effects of depression.

MYTH: If you ignore it, it will go away.

FACT: Mild depression may go away with time, but if depression persists for more than two weeks one should seek psychotherapy and understanding or perhaps medical help in the form of one of the many antidepressants.

MYTH: People who talk about suicide would never do it.

FACT: Those who have contemplated suicide have dropped subtle and obvious hints in various ways.

MYTH: Depression is simply sadness.

FACT: Depression is an illness because it works against healing.

Signs of Depression

There seem to be two consistent symptoms of depression. One is the loss of interest and pleasure in usual activities (anhedonia) and a relative persistent disturbance of mood (dysphoria). Other signals may be:

- Persistent feelings of sadness or irritability.
- Persistent and uncontrollable crying spells.
- Loss of interest in pleasurable activities such as hobbies or sex.
- A change of weight or appetite.
- A change in sleep pattern—especially waking up in the middle of the night.
- Feelings of helplessness and hopelessness.
- Loss of energy and motivation.
- Decreased ability to concentrate.
- Signs of dementia.
- Decline of self-esteem.
- Increase in complaining and pessimism.
- Fear of failure or success.
- Statements such as: "What's the use," "I'm in the way," "I am worthless," "I would be better off dead."
- Thoughts of death or suicide.

Helping Yourself

Be patient and gentle with yourself. If depression is a result of a loss or grief, with care it will run its course. Life will become meaningful again.

Remember, only people who do not care avoid suffering from this kind of depression.

Seek professional help to assist in sorting through and understanding the cause or causes of your depression. Dealing with depression by not dealing with it is the worst option available. Depression not only has a cause, it usually has a purpose. To understand this is to grow and to grow through depression somehow makes the pain more tolerable.

Many times medication is the answer. When medicine is the answer, it should be used.

Make a contract with your significant other to carry the load, if and when you become depressed, by seeking professional help and ensuring the pursuit of a healthy lifestyle while you are unmotivated to do so on your own.

The more you are exposed to light-hearted things, such as beautiful sights and sounds and laughter, the more uplifting this is to your spirit.

During winter months, seek as much sunlight as possible to minimize seasonal affective disorder. Full spectrum artificial light is believed to help.

One of the greatest antidotes to depression is giving. Seek always ways in which to give of your time, your talents, and your money. "Blessed are those who give."

UNDERSTANDING GRIEF

Grief is an emotional and physical reaction to a significant loss. Grief is typically understood to result from the death of a loved one. However, grief results from any meaningful loss. Such experiences as divorce, loss of a home, loss of a job or career, loss of a body part, and empty nest are all momentous losses that are felt on the personal level. Grief is the process in which one adjusts and works through the difficult feelings following the loss. Grief is emotional in that feelings range from fear to anger, guilt, depression, and even hope. Uncontrollable crying and anxiety may accompany mourning. Grief is physical in that it may affect appetite and sleep patterns, cause headaches and other body pains, nausea, and even compromise the immune system.

Grief is very misunderstood in our society. Since grief is a consequence of death, dying, and personal losses, many tend to ignore and avoid the subject. Even some professionals such as clergy and physicians are sometimes ill advised on such issues as healthy/unhealthy grief reactions and typical/atypical time frame for grief.

Even though grief can be painful, there are no quick fixes. One must not seek to avoid any of the stages; rather, seek to experience all the phases of grief and grow through the experience.

Most professionals maintain that the reorganization and adjustment to a significant loss takes from eighteen to twenty-four months.

Life is like an onion, you peel off one layer at a time, and sometimes you weep.

Carl Sandburg

Some of the Life Events That Cause Grief

Loss of a Loved One

- Through death
- Terminal illness
- Disappearance or alienation
- Divorce or ended relationship
- Miscarriage or abortion
- Empty nest
- Moving away
- Death of pet

Loss of Personal Item

- Prized keepsake
- Amputation of body part
- Mental or physical function
- Bankruptcy

Loss of Place

- Fire or disaster
- Moving

Loss of Position

- Losing job
- Inability to function in profession
- Retirement
- Loss of status or power

Stages of Grief

According to Elisabeth Kübler-Ross, MD (1970), a pioneer researcher in the field of death and loss, there are several identifiable stages of grief.

- Shock and numbness
- Denial
- Anger
- Depression
- Bargaining
- Acceptance

Even though these stages or phases of grief are recognizable to those familiar with grief work, the stages are usually manifested with personal expressions. Since feelings are often disguised in questions and in tears, it is not uncommon for these or similar statements to be used.

- "This can't be happening to me."—denial
- "Why me?"—anger
- "Woe is me."—depression
- "Let's you and me . . ."—bargaining

Acute or unresolved grief may result in body (somatic) distress.

- General aches and pains
- Digestive problems
- Shortness of breath
- Weight change
- Accident proneness
- Compromised immune system

Change in Lifestyle Patterns

- Sleep
- Eating
- Sex
- Daily routines

Delusional Thinking

- See/hear/smell the deceased
- Preoccupation with the image of the deceased
- Develop traits and symptoms of the deceased

Emotional Distress

- Hostility
- Lethargy
- Depression
- Guilt
- Feeling of "going crazy"
- Inability to concentrate and make decisions

Grief is normal and healthy in that it is a normal response to a personal loss. It is the slow and often painful reorganizing of life after a significant loss. This adjustment is not invited, yet the ability to endure and even grow through grief is a universal experience.

Helpful Hints

- Join a grief support group.
- Be a part of healing and support to others.
- Turn to your religious tradition.
- Volunteer in your community.
- Realize that pets may be great companions.
- Be honest with your feelings.
- Be gentle and patient with yourself.
- Accept that at some level your loss has changed you.
- Remember, time plus love fosters healing.

Endings happen—so do beginnings.

The Serenity Prayer

> God grant me the serenity
> To accept the things I cannot change,
> Courage to change the things I can,
> And wisdom to know the difference.

UNDERSTANDING INDIVIDUAL UNIQUENESS

A hallmark of our government is that all citizens are intended to have equal rights. This is not to imply, however, that all are equally alike. If every snowflake is different, why should we be surprised to learn that this is true for humans, too? Yet, people are often astonished to learn that others are not just like them. No one can ever think, feel, understand, or even see and hear what another uniquely experiences. All people are different.

There are as many personalities as there are people. An individual's temperament or personality is as unique as his or her fingerprints. Even identical twins possess their own individuality. From these fundamental differences come particular values, needs, motives, impulses, thoughts, feelings, and actions. To try and change someone fundamentally will be a pursuit of frustrating experiences. Nonetheless, not accepting others for who they are is more prevalent than we may think.

Differences in temperament was first presented by Hipprocates about 2,500 years ago. His personality types—choleric, phlegmatic, melancholic, and sanguine—are still referred to today. Sigmund Freud differentiated the human drive into three categories: the id, the ego, and the superego. One of Freud's contemporaries, Carl Jung, broadened this model in the 1920s by saying that people are driven by a multitude of instincts which he called archetypes. Isabel Myers and her mother Katherine Briggs expanded Jung's psychological types into sixteen temperaments. Interestingly, the four predominate categories of the sixteen Myers-Briggs types fall neatly into the four temperaments of Hipprocates.

Eric Berne, the founder of transactional analysis (TA), found it useful to understand human behavior by labeling three distinct ego states that stimulate, motivate, monitor, and control. Berne called these three ego states:

- Parent—which could be nurturing or critical.
- Adult—which comes from an equal nonjudgmental perspective.
- Child—which is expressed as adaptive or free child.

Every response that one makes is from one of these ego states and is directed to one of these states in another. Analyzing communication exchanges in this way reveals much about human behavior and our uniqueness.

Richard Bandler and John Grinder, the developers of neuro-linguistic programming (NLP), discovered that people receive, store, and retrieve information and create new ideas by using one of their senses in a predominate way. The three basic representational systems are:

- Visual—relating to pictures and images.
- Auditory—based on sounds and words.
- Kinesthetic—pertaining to sensations and feelings.

One's choice of words, eye movement, and learning channels reveal his or her primary NLP style. Understanding the style of others may better prevent misunderstandings and promote rapport. One style certainly is not preferred over another. Yet, appreciating these fundamental human differences can re-move many unnecessary obstacles.

Human Differences Are Infinite

Some are:	While others are:
Extroverted	Introverted
Congruent	Inconsistent
Nervous	Composed
Positive	Negative
Hostile	Tolerant
Self-disciplined	Impulsive
Expressive	Inhibited
Sympathetic	Indifferent
Subjective	Objective
Big	Small
Submissive	Dominant
Trusting	Suspicious
Forthright	Shrewd
Conservative	Liberal
Leader	Follower
Tense	Relaxed
Dependent	Independent
Left brain	Right brain
Healthy	Ill
Immature	Wise
Spiritual	Agnostic
Rigid	Flexible
Male	Female
Yin	Yang

Myths Prevail

- All men are alike.
- That is just the way women are.
- If you've seen one (ethnic group, race, religious group), you've seen them all.

To understand another is to appreciate the differences. May these differences be prized and cherished and not ridiculed or condemned.

Seek always to implement the Golden Rule: "Do unto others as you would have them do unto you."

UNDERSTANDING MARRIAGE PROBLEMS

Marriages are universal. Everyone knows what a marriage is supposed to look like—right? Actually, answers may simply encapsulate personal experience. Or, one's understanding of marriage is guided by his or her paradigm. Realistically every marriage is unique. Yet, regardless of one's definition, most will agree that there are times when marriages have problems.

Just as when driving on a good interstate highway with no curves, hills, or obstacles, one still has to make steering and acceleration corrections—so it is in a good marriage. Corrections must be made and homeostasis maintained. When a problem is left unaddressed and erosion begins, it will, if ignored, eventually eat away the fundamentals which originally nourished the relationship. It is similar to cutting away the vegetation on a hillside. Without the network of roots holding the soil in place, erosion eventually prevents the growth of virtually all plant life. So it is when couples become invested in anger instead of caring, and erosion is allowed to continue in a relationship.

It may be shocking to know that what draws couples together is often the thing that drives them apart. Initially, couples are attracted to each other because of some fundamentals that they share in common. This may include factors such as shared age category, same race, common values, and similar social class. After basic commonalities are shared, couples move to a commitment phase because of complementary traits, which offer balance. At this level, opposites attract. The opposite traits may include one being a talker and the other quiet. One may be intuitive and the other sensing. One may be predominantly thinking and the other predominantly feeling. One perhaps is dominant and the other is submissive. One may be logical and systematic while the other is imaginative and creative. In this regard, each may be more complete and well rounded with his or her opposite offering balance. The opposite is intriguing if not mystical. At the same time, however, one's opposite can be complicated if not confusing. Definitely a potential for a problem in a relationship.

Is your relationship?

- Disengaged—and you are living separate lives
- Connected—yet minimal shared experiences
- Enmeshed—and have little personal identity or space
- Engaged—with healthy blending and individuation

Myths Prevail

- Now that we're married, we don't have to work on our relationship.
- We will live on love.
- My spouse should make me happy.

- I can change my spouse.
- Good marriages are trouble free.
- If I ignore my emotions, they will go away.
- If I ignore our problems, they will go away.
- A relationship "locks in" and need not change.
- I'm nothing like my parents.
- I won't do things the way my parents did.

Common Causes of Marital Conflict

- Ignoring initial signs of incompatibility
- Lack of communication
- Lack of intimacy
- Substance abuse
- Personality clashes
- Psychological problems
- Health problems
- Third-person entanglements
- Loss of trust
- Crisis produced from family developmental stage
- Crisis produced from an external/situational event
- Disagreements on how to raise children
- Financial problems
- Sexual incompatibility
- In-law conflicts
- Career commitments
- Loss of shared interests and goals
- Blaming instead of taking responsibility

When Difficulties Occur, What Can I Do?

- Realize there are no quick fixes.
- Seek to understand as well as be understood.
- Seek to hear the feelings behind the words.
- Seek ways to strengthen communication.
- Seek to be more affirming and accepting of each other.
- Seek ways to express your commitment to each other.
- Seek to be specific with your wants and needs.
- Seek to verbalize the unspoken rules.
- Seek a minivacation for a change of pace.
- Seek to laugh with your spouse every day.
- Seek to learn about your (and your spouse's) temperament.
- Seek to develop your faith and spiritual understanding.

- Seek out marriage enrichment opportunities periodically.
- Seek professional counseling when your marriage is in trouble.
- Realize that you did not get into a crisis overnight and you will not get out of it in a day.

It is common to seek professional help from lawyers, physicians, and financial advisors. Why be reluctant to seek out professional help with marriage problems?

UNDERSTANDING MONEY TROUBLES

Most all of us have had financial pressures at one time or another. We live in a materialistic world where money is power and spending is a status symbol. Lifestyles are such that just staying dry in a cave is quite insufficient. Money is the means to acquire the goods and services we want and need. However, money has come to influence how we feel about ourselves and others. More money is nice, but it is not the answer. Controlling our resources is. Those who "have" and those who "have not" cannot be determined solely by how much is earned. Distinctions can be made, however, by how one manages his or her resources. A sense of control of our resources promotes personal satisfaction and contentment. Indeed, it is the responsible management of our resources that leads to happiness.

Each day Americans are overwhelmed by media blitzes and commercials designed to separate them from their money. To surrender the control of one's money is to lose control of one's finances.

Did you know that $3,000 charged on a credit card with a finance charge rate of 18 percent, and paying the minimum payments, would take thirty years to pay off, and would cost $13,276 in interest?

Ask Yourself

- Could I pay my bills if I was not paid for a month?
- Do I know how much money I owe to my creditors?
- Do I have a budget? Is it realistic?
- Does it reflect my values?

Financial Stress Happens

- Loss or reduction of income
- Major illness or disability
- Divorce
- Death in the family
- Major repair

- College expenses
- Other crisis
- Overextended in purchasing

Signs of a Problem

Do you:

- Routinely spend more than you earn
- Rob Peter to pay Paul
- Max the limit of credit cards
- Skip paying some bills to pay others
- Borrow more money to pay off bills

Some are better money managers than others, but no one is born with the ability to manage money effectively. Money management is a skill—it requires learning and practice.

Dealing with financial problems puts one in contact with values. Not just the values of smart shopping, but the values that shape lives and give life its meaning.

Managing your money, as opposed to letting it control you, creates a good feeling which fosters confidence, self-esteem, and peace of mind.

Simply having money doesn't prevent one from worrying or even obsessing about it. Money anxiety says more about how we feel about ourselves than it does about our bank balances.

To fail to plan is to plan to fail.

Develop a plan to:

- Live within your income
- Realize personal goals
- Maintain a good credit history
- Get more for your money
- Reduce financial stress and arguments
- Achieve competence and confidence

UNDERSTANDING STRESS

Stress is like blood pressure in the sense that we all need some, we just don't want it to get too high. Put simply, stress is the way you react to change. This reaction can be measured physically and felt emotionally. Stress can be positive (eustress) when it helps you focus, concentrate, and reach peak efficiency. Stress becomes negative (distress) when you stay "geared up," "psyched up," or overwhelmed with change. In any case, it is possible to learn how to manage stress and channel this energy into a more positive outcome.

Stress is an unavoidable part of life, but it doesn't have to be a chronic way of life. Anxiety results from acute peaks of stress. Burnout is the total lack of motivation which can result from prolonged and overwhelming stress.

We live in an increasingly changing world. You cannot always control the change, but you can control your response to it.

Types of Stress

Life Cycle

Infancy
Childhood
Adolescence
Marriage
Pregnancy
Parenthood
Job demands
Divorce
Empty nest
Death of spouse, family member, other
Senior years

Physical

Disability
Injury
Addictions

Personal

Attitudes about yourself—like/dislike, capable/incapable
Feelings—anger, fear, anxiety, guilt
Expectations of others—friendly/hostile, helpful/harmful

Social

Inflation/recession
Technology
Unemployment

Changing values
Relocation
Travel
Urban problems
Energy crisis

Job

Job dissatisfaction
Conflict—with supervisors, co-workers
Work overload
Monotony
Time pressures
Unclear expectations
Public attitudes

Good and Bad Stress

Think about three stresses you encounter frequently that are good for you and three that are bad for you. Write them down. By labeling stress in this way you should be better prepared to recognize stressors as they occur and thus be better prepared to manage personal stress.

Signs of Stress

- General irritability
- Pounding of the heart
- Chest pain
- Dryness of the mouth
- Impulsive behavior
- Overpowering urge to cry or run and hide
- Inability to concentrate
- Feelings of unreality, weakness, or dizziness
- Fatigue
- Floating anxiety
- Emotional tension and alertness
- Trembling, nervous tics
- Tendency to be easily startled by small sounds, etc.
- High-pitched, nervous laughter
- Stuttering and other speech difficulties
- Grinding of the teeth
- Sleep problems
- Hyperactivity

- Sweating
- Frequent need to urinate
- Diarrhea, indigestion, queasiness, and even vomiting
- Headaches
- Low back and neck pain
- Premenstrual tension or missed cycles
- Loss of or excessive appetite
- Increased smoking, alcohol, or drugs
- Nightmares
- Emotional instability
- Irrational behavior
- Accident proneness

When Stress Is Not Managed

Uncontrolled stress is not only distressing, it may contribute to a stroke, coronary disease, cancer, lung ailments, cirrhosis of the liver, and an impaired immune system.

When Stress Is Managed

Stress, when properly identified and channeled, is one of life's most positive energies. Stress sometimes reveals opportunities for making mid-course corrections in our lives. Stress is good when it fuels performance, enhances creativity, and stimulates performance beyond natural capabilities.

Many times stress leads to clarifying values and releasing creative energy for personal growth that makes life healthier and more meaningful.

Ways to Manage Stress

- Treat yourself with kindness and respect.
- Take time and find a spot to be quiet and peaceful.
- Aerobic exercise is a must to burn off the adrenaline that stress introduces and create calming chemicals.
- Eat a balanced, nutritional diet.
- Learn to do deep breathing exercises.
- Engage in relaxation exercises.
- Practice positive visualization. Picture yourself in your most positive way.
- Laugh more.
- Avoid excessive alcohol or "quick fix" drugs.

- Give support, encouragement, and praise to others. Learn to accept it in return.
- Focus on the good in your life.
- Resolve to grow.
- Celebrate your transcendent self. Your spirit strives to love and be loved.

References

Preface

Clinebell, Howard (1981). *Contemporary Growth Therapies*. Nashville, TN: Abingdon Press.

Chapter 1

American Association of Pastoral Counselors (2000). *Pastoral Counseling: A Mental Health Resource*. Fairfax, VA. Advisory Committee on Advocacy, James Wyrtzen, Chairperson and American Association of Pastoral Counselors, C. Roy Woodruff, Executive Director.

VandeCreek, Larry and Laurel Burton (2001). *Professional Chaplaincy: Its Role and Importance In Health Care*. The Association for Clinical Pastoral Education. The Association of Professional Chaplains. The Canadian Association of Pastoral Practice and Education. The National Association of Catholic Chaplains. The National Association of Jewish Chaplains.

Veroff, Joseph, Richard Kulka, and Elizabeth Dorran (1981). *Mental Health in America: Patterns of Help-Seeking from 1957-1976*. New York: Basic Books.

Woodruff, Roy (2001). "New national survey powerfully affirms desire for pastoral counseling." *Currents* 39, p. 2.

Chapter 2

Chopra, Deepak (1991). *Unconditional Life: Mastering the Forces that Shape Personal Reality*. New York: Bantam Books.

Davenberg, Richard V. and Mark Braverman (1999). *The Violence Prone Workplace: A New Approach to Dealing with Hostile, Threatening, and Uncivil Behavior*. Ithaca, NY: Cornell University Press.

Delattre, Edwin J. (1984). Ethics in the information age. *Public Relations Journal*. June, p. 12.

Harris, Thomas A. (1973). *I'm OK—You're OK*. New York: Avon Books.

Kaufer, Steve and Jurg W. Mattman (2001). *The Cost of Workplace Violence to American Business*. Palm Springs, CA: Workplace Violence Research Institute.

Luks, Allan (1992). *The Healing Power of Doing Good*. New York: Fawcett Columbine.

Menz, Robert L. (1997). *A Memoir of a Pastoral Counseling Practice.* Binghamton, NY: The Haworth Press.

National Institute for Occupational Safety and Health (1997). *Violence in the Workplace: Risk Factors and Prevention Strategies.* Current Intelligence Bulletin 57. Cincinnati, OH: NIOSH.

Nye, Sandra (1998). *Employee Assistance Law Desk Book.* Arlington, VA: Employee Assistance Professionals Association.

Peck, M. Scott (1987). *The Different Drum: Community-Making and Peace.* New York: Simon and Schuster.

Sygnatur, Eric F. and Guy A. Toscano (2000). *Work Related Homicides: The Facts.* Compensation and Working Conditions Volume 5, Number 1. Washington, DC: Bureau of Labor Statistics.

Tischler, Henry L. (2002). *Introduction to Sociology,* Seventh Edition. Fort Worth, TX: Harcourt.

U.S. Census Bureau (1996). *Statistical Abstract of the United States,* 116th Edition. Washington, DC: U.S. Government Printing Office.

Chapter 3

Alcoholics Anonymous (1976). *Alcoholics Anonymous,* Third Edition. New York: Alcoholics Anonymous World Services, Inc.

American Institute of Stress (2000). *Stress—America's #1 Health Problem.* Yonkers, NY: Author.

American Psychiatric Association (2000). *Diagnostic and Statistical Manual of Mental Disorders,* Fourth Edition. Washington, DC: Author.

Anderson, Gerald F. (1997). "In search of value: An international comparison of cost, access, and outcomes." *Health Affairs* 16(6), pp. 163-171.

Bennefield, Robert L. (1998). *Health Insurance Coverage: 1997.* Washington, DC: U.S. Bureau of the Census.

Burton, Wayne N. and Daniel J. Conti (1999). The real measure of productivity. *Business and Health* 17(11), pp. 34-36.

Dayringer, Richard (1995). *Dealing with Depression.* Binghamton, NY: The Haworth Press.

Depression Guideline Panel (1993). *Clinical Practice Guideline Number 5: Depression in Primary Care. Volume 1: Detection and Diagnosis.* Rockville, MD: Agency for Health Care Policy and Research. U.S. Department of Health and Human Services, AHCPR publication 93-0550.

Greenberg, Paul (1999). Tackling costs one disease at a time. *Business and Health* 17(5), pp. 31-37.

Greenberg, P. E., L. E. Stiglin, S. N. Finkelstein, and E. R. Berndt (1993). The economic burden of depression in 1990. *Journal of Clinical Psychiatry* 54, pp. 405-418.

Hafer, Fred D. (1998). The cost of doing nothing. *EAPA Exchange* 28(1), p. 17.

Jung, C. J. (1963). *Mysterium Coniunctionis, Collected Works,* Volume 14, translated by R. F. C. Hull. New York: Pantheon.

Klier, Barbara A., Jacquelyn F. Quiram, and Mark Siegel (Eds.) (1999). *Alcohol and Tobacco—America's Drug of Choice.* Wylie, TX: Information Plus.

Levit, Katherine R. (1997). National health expenditures, 1996. *Health Care Financing Review* 19(1), pp. 161-200.

Manderscheid, R. W. and M. A. Sonnenschein (1994). *Mental Health, United States, 1994.* Washington, DC: Center for Mental Health Services.

Menz, Robert L. (1997). *A Memoir of a Pastoral Counseling Practice.* Binghamton, NY: The Haworth Press.

National Institute for Occupational Safety and Health (1996). *National Occupational Research Agenda.* Publication Number 96-115. Cincinnati, OH: NIOSH.

National Institute on Alcohol Abuse and Alcoholism (1998). *Alcohol Alert.* No. 42: October. Rockville, MD: NIAAA.

National Institute on Alcohol Abuse and Alcoholism (2001). *Alcohol Alert.* No. 51: January. Rockville, MD: NIAAA.

Northwestern National Life—Employee Benefits Division (1991). *Employee Burnout: America's Newest Epidemic.* Minneapolis, MN: The North Atlantic Life Insurance Company of America, New York, NY.

Power, Robert D. and Frederick Y. Fung (1994). *Workers' Compensation Handbook.* San Diego, CA: K. W. Publications.

Prentice, Thomas (1999). World Health Report, WHO, Geneva, Switzerland. <http://www.who.int>.

Regier, Darrel A. (1993). The de facto U.S. mental and addictive disorders service system. *Archives of General Psychiatry,* 50 (February), pp. 85-94.

Stamler, Rose (1999). Preventing cardiovascular disease: Addressing the nation's leading killer. Centers for Disease Control and Prevention. <http://www.cdc.gov/nccdphp>.

Trice, Harrison M. and Paul M. Roman (1972). *Spirits and Demons at Work: Alcohol and Other Drugs on the Job.* Ithaca, NY: New York State School of Industrial and Labor Relations, Cornell University.

U.S. Department of Health and Human Services (1999). *Mental Health: A Report of the Surgeon General.* Rockville, MD: U.S. Department of Health and Human Services, Substance Abuse and Mental Health Services Administration, Center for Mental Health Services, National Institutes of Health, National Institute of Mental Health.

Viscott, David (1992). *Emotionally Free.* Chicago, IL: Contemporary Books.

Wexler, Barbara (2003). *Health and Wellness: Illness Among Americans.* Farmington Hills, MI: Thomson Gale.

Williams, Redford, and Virginia Williams (1994). *Anger Kills: Seventeen Strategies for Controlling the Hostility That Can Harm Your Health.* New York: Harper Perennial.

Chapter 4

Cousins, Norman (1979). *The Anatomy of an Illness As Perceived by the Patient.* New York: Bantam Books.

Cousins, Norman (1989). *Head First: The Biology of Hope.* New York: E. P. Dunton.

Descartes, René (1911). *The Philosophical Works of Descartes,* translated by Elizabeth S. Haldane and G. R. T. Ross. London: Cambridge University Press.

Erikson, Erik H. (1968). *Identity: Youth and Crisis.* New York: W. W. Norton.

Faber, Heije (1977). *Pastoral Care in the Modern Hospital.* Philadelphia, PA: The Westminster Press.

Fine, Reuben (1988). *Troubled Men.* San Francisco: Jossey-Bass Inc., Publishers.

Harlow, H. F. (1959). Love in infant monkeys. *Scientific American* 200(6), pp. 68-74.

Harris, Thomas A. (1973). *I'm OK—You're OK.* New York: Avon Books.

Hay, Louise L. (1982). *Heal Your Body.* Carlsbad, CA: Hay House, Inc.

Hay, Louise L. (1984). *You Can Heal Your Life.* Carlsbad, CA: Hay House, Inc.

Ingelfinger, Franz (1980). Arrogance. *New England Journal of Medicine* 303, pp. 1506-1511.

Office of Disease Prevention and Health Promotion, U.S. Department of Health and Human Services (2000). *Healthy People 2000 Fact Sheet.* <http://odphp.osophs.dhhs.gov/pubs/hp2000>.

Robbins, John (1996). *Reclaiming Our Health.* Tiburon, CA: H. J. Kramer, Inc.

Simonton, O. Carl, Stephanie Matthews-Simonton, and James Creighton (1978). *Getting Well Again.* Los Angeles, CA: J. P. Tarcher, Inc.

Steiner, Claude M. (1974). *Scripts People Live.* New York: Bantam Books.

U.S. Department of Health and Human Services, Public Health Service (1990). *Healthy People 2000: National Health Promotion and Disease Prevention Objectives.* Washington, DC: DHHS, PHS.

World Health Organization (1948). Preamble to the Constitution of the World Health Organization as adopted by the International Health Conference, New York, 19-22 June, 1946; signed on 22 July 1946 by the representatives of 61 States (Official Records of the World Health Organization, no. 2, p. 100) and entered into force on 7 April 1948.

Chapter 5

Ban Breathnach, Sarah (1995). *Simple Abundance: A Daybook of Comfort and Joy.* New York: Warner Books.

Byrd, Randolph C. (1998). Positive therapeutic effects of intercessory prayer in a coronary care unit population. *Southern Medical Journal* 81(7), pp. 826-829.

Cannon, W. B. (1932). *The Wisdom of the Body.* New York: W. W. Norton.

Dossey, Larry (1993). *Healing Words: The Power of Prayer and the Practice of Medicine.* New York: HarperCollins Publishers.

Dossey, Larry (1996). *Prayer Is Good Medicine.* New York: HarperCollins Publishers.

Holmes, T. H. and R. H. Rahe (1967a). The social readjustment rating scale. *Journal of Psychosomatic Research* 11, pp. 213-218.

Holmes, T. H. and R. H. Rahe (1967b). Survey: Schedule of recent experience (SRE). Department of Psychiatry, University of Washington School of Medicine.

Koenig, Harold G. (1997). *Is Religion Good for Your Health? The Effects of Religion on Physical and Mental Health.* Binghamton, NY: The Haworth Press.

Pelletier, Kenneth R. (1992). *Mind As Healer, Mind As Slayer.* New York: Dell Publishing.

Princeton Religion Research Center (1996). "Religion in America: Will the vitality of the church be the surprise of the 21st century?" Princeton, NJ: Gallup Poll.

Selye, H. (1950). *The Physiology and Pathology of Exposure to Stress.* Montreal, Canada: Acta.

Chapter 6

Chopra, Deepak (1993). *Ageless Body, Timeless Mind.* New York: Harmony Books.

Frankl, Victor E. (1977). *Man's Search for Meaning.* New York: Pocket Books.

National Center for Complementary and Alternative Medicine (2002). *NCCAM Funding: Appropriations History.* Bethesda, MD: NCCAM, National Institutes of Health.

Pelletier, Kenneth R. (1994). *Sound Mind, Sound Body.* New York: Simon and Schuster.

Weil, Andrew. (1995). *Spontaneous Healing.* New York: Fawcett Columbine.

World Health Organization (1948). Preamble to the Constitution of the World Health Organization as adopted by the International Health Conference, New York, 19-22 June, 1946; signed on 22 July 1946 by the representatives of 61 States (Official Records of the World Health Organization, no. 2, p. 100) and entered into force on 7 April 1948.

Appendix

Alters, Sandra (2000). *Alcohol and Tobacco, America's Drugs of Choice.* Farmington Hills, MI: Thomson Gale.

Daugherty, Roy and Terry O'Bryan (1990). *The Talking About Alcohol and Drugs Series.* Lexington, KY: Prevention Research Institute.

Haynes, Thomas (1988). The changing role of the physician in the treatment of chemical dependence. The history of addiction medicine. Presented in Minneapolis, MN, October 1988. <www.wemac.com/adm_hist.html>.

Klier, Barbara A., Jacquelyn F. Quiram, and Mark Siegel (Eds.) (1999). *Alcohol and Tobacco—America's Drug of Choice.* Wylie, TX: Information Plus.

Kübler-Ross, Elisabeth (1970). *On Death and Dying.* New York: Macmillan.
National Institute of Alcohol Abuse and Alcoholism (2001). *Alcohol Alert,* No. 51: January. Rockville, MD: NIAAA.
National Institute on Drug Abuse (1999). National Household Survey on Drug Abuse: Main findings 1997. April 1999. Bethesda, MD: NIDA, National Institutes of Health.

Index

National Association of Catholic
 Chaplains, 5
National Association of Jewish
 Chaplains, 5
National Council on Alcoholism and
 Drug Dependence, 125
National Institute for Occupational
 Safety and Health (NIOSH),
 23, 43
National Institute on Alcohol Abuse
 and Alcoholism (NIAAA), 58
National Institutes of Health (NIH),
 105
National Safe Workplace Institute, 23
Neuro-linguistic programming (NLP),
 138
NIAAA, 58
Niebuhr, Reinhold, 87
NIH, 105
NIOSH, 23, 43
NLP, 138
Nutrition, 52, 109-111

Occupational Safety and Health Act, 43
Orman, Suze, 95

Paradigm shift
 benefits, 13-14
 holistic view of health, 12
 levels of health intervention
  behavioral prevention, 13
  medical intervention, 12
  pro-wellness, 13
  structural prevention, 12-13
Pastoral Care in the Modern Hospital
 (Faber), 64
*Pastoral Counseling: A National
 Mental Health Resource*
 (American Association of
 Pastoral Counselors), 8
Pastoral counselors, 7-8
Peale, Norman Vincent, 7, 85
Peck, M. Scott, 8, 29, 30, 95

Pelletier, Kenneth R., 91, 100-101
Physical birth, 77
Physical exercise, 111-113
Positive outlook, 72
Positive thinking, 85
Prayer, 108-109. *See also* Meditation
Presenteeism, 41
*Professional Chaplaincy: Its Role and
 Importance in Health Care*
 (VandeCreek and Burton), 5
Program models, 8-9
Prohibition, 58
Psyche, 121
Psychergonomics
 awareness of, 37-61
  alcohol abuse, 57-60
  anger, 55-57
  cost of health care, 39-40
  depression, 49-52
  emotional stress, 52-55
  factors affecting health, 37-38
  leading causes of death, 38-39
  mental illness, 46-49
  moving toward, 43-46
  wellness and corporate setting,
   40-43
 defined, 3, 10-11
 prevention as key to, 10
 principles of wellness, 81
Psychological birth, 77
Psychoneuroimmunology, 89-90
Psychotherapy, as treatment for
 depression, 51

Quiram, Jacquelyn F., 58

Rahe, Richard, 86-87
Reclaiming Our Health (Robbins), 70
Redfield, James, 95
Regier, Darrel A., 47
Relaxation, 113-116
Robbins, John, 70
Rolfing, 106

SAD, 52, 132
Samaritan Institute, 4
Satcher, David, 47-49
Schulz, Charles, 49
Seasonal affective disorder (SAD), 52,
　132
Selye, Hans, 91
Serenity prayer, 137
Siegel, Bernie, 95
Siegel, Mark, 58
Simonton, O. Carl, 71
Social birth, 77
Social Readjustment Rating Scale,
　86-87
Sonnenschein, M. A., 47
Sound Mind, Sound Body Project,
　100-101
Spirit. *See* Mind-body-spirit
Spirits and Demons at Work (Trice and
　Roman), 58-59
Spirituality, increasing interest in, 3-4
Spontaneous Healing (Weil), 105
Stamler, Rose, 38
Steiner, Claude M., 77
Stress. *See* Emotional stress
Stroking, 77
Supplements, 110-111

TA, 138
Thanatos, 107
Therapeutic touch, 106
Thirteenth Century Chronicle
　(Salimbene), 79
Tischler, Henry, 22
Tranquilizers, 87
Transactional analysis (TA), 138
Twelve steps, 60

Unconditional Life (Chopra), 33

Van Gogh, Vincent, 49
VandeCreek, Larry, 5

Violence in the workplace
　characteristics of violent offenders,
　　26-27
　correlation with violence in media,
　　21-22
　defined, 23-24
　prevention strategies, 24-25
　seeds of, 21
　suggestions for managers, 25-26
　workplace homicides, 22-23, 24
Viscott, David, 52
Volstead Act, 58

Wallace, Mike, 49
Weil, Andrew, 95, 105, 113
Wellness
　affirmation, acceptance, and, 77-80
　body messages, 68-70
　change in health industry, 70-72
　interconnectedness, 64-67
　nonholistic understanding of health,
　　63-64
　power of words, 67-68
　practicing, 99-119
　　alternative and complementary
　　　forms, 105-116
　　healthy models for, 100-104
　　holistic, 116-118
　　incentives, 119
　　self-awareness and, 104-105
　proactive for, 80-81
　psychergonomic principles of, 81
　secondary gains of illness, 73-77
WHO, 80, 100-101
Wholeness. *See also*
　　Interconnectedness
　defined, 83-84
　importance of, 3
Williams, Redford, 56
Williams, Virginia, 56
Williamson, Marianne, 95
Woodruff, Roy, 4
Worker Productivity Index (WPI), 41
Workers' compensation, 43-44

World Health Organization (WHO), 80,
        100-101
WPI, 41
Wright, Dale, 50

You Can Heal Your Life (Hay), 66

Zukov, Gary, 95

THE HAWORTH PASTORAL PRESS®
Pastoral Care, Ministry, and Spirituality
Richard Dayringer, ThD
Senior Editor

A PASTORAL COUNSELOR'S MODEL FOR WELLNESS IN THE WORK-PLACE: PSYCHERGONOMICS by Robert L. Menz. "This text is a 'must' read for chaplains and pastoral counselors wishing to understand and apply holistic health care to troubled employees, whether they be nurses, physicians, other health care workers, or workers in other industries. This book is filled with practical ideas and tools to help clergy care for the physical, mental, and spiritual needs of employees at the workplace." *Harold G. Koenig, MD, Associate Professor of Psychiatry, Duke University Medical Center; Author,* Chronic Pain: Biomedical and Spiritual Approaches

A THEOLOGY OF PASTORAL PSYCHOTHERAPY: GOD'S PLAY IN SACRED SPACES by Brian W. Grant. "Brian Grant's book is a compassionate and sophisticated synthesis of theology and psychoanalysis. His wise, warm grasp binds a community of healers with the personal qualities, responsibilities, and burdens of the pastoral psychotherapist." *David E. Scharff, MD, Co-Director, International Institute of Object Relations Therapy*

LOSSES IN LATER LIFE: A NEW WAY OF WALKING WITH GOD, SECOND EDITION by R. Scott Sullender. "Continues to be a timely and helpful book. There is an empathetic tone throughout, even though the book is a bold challenge to grieve for the sake of growth and maturity and faithfulness. . . . An important book." *Herbert Anderson, PhD, Professor of Pastoral Theology, Catholic Theological Union, Chicago, Illinois*

CARING FOR PEOPLE FROM BIRTH TO DEATH edited by James E. Hightower Jr. "An expertly detailed account of the hopes and hazards folks experience at each stage of their lives. Your empathy will be deepened and your care of people will be highly informed." *Wayne E. Oates, PhD, Professor of Psychiatry Emeritus, School of Medicine, University of Louisville, Kentucky*

HIDDEN ADDICTIONS: A PASTORAL RESPONSE TO THE ABUSE OF LEGAL DRUGS by Bridget Clare McKeever. "This text is a must–read for physicians, pastors, nurses, and counselors. It should be required reading in every seminary and Clinical Pastoral Education program." *Martin C. Helldorfer, DMin, Vice President, Mission, Leadership Development and Corporate Culture, Catholic Health Initiatives—Eastern Region, Pennsylvania*

THE EIGHT MASKS OF MEN: A PRACTICAL GUIDE IN SPIRITUAL GROWTH FOR MEN OF THE CHRISTIAN FAITH by Frederick G. Grosse. "Thoroughly grounded in traditional Christian spirituality and thoughtfully aware of the needs of men in our culture. . . . Close attention could make men's groups once again a vital spiritual force in the church." *Eric O. Springsted, PhD, Chaplain and Professor of Philosophy and Religion, Illinois College, Jacksonville, Illinois*

THE HEART OF PASTORAL COUNSELING: HEALING THROUGH RELATION-SHIP, REVISED EDITION by Richard Dayringer. "Richard Dayringer's revised edition of *The Heart of Pastoral Counseling* is a book for every person's pastor and a pastor's every person." *Glen W. Davidson, Professor, New Mexico Highlands University, Las Vegas, New Mexico*

WHEN LIFE MEETS DEATH: STORIES OF DEATH AND DYING, TRUTH AND COURAGE by Thomas W. Shane. "A kaleidoscope of compassionate, artfully tendered pastoral encounters that evoke in the reader a full range of emotions." *The Rev. Dr. James M. Harper, III, Corporate Director of Clinical Pastoral Education, Health Midwest; Director of Pastoral Care, Baptist Medical Center and Research Medical Center, Kansas City Missouri*

A MEMOIR OF A PASTORAL COUNSELING PRACTICE by Robert L. Menz. "Challenges the reader's belief system. A humorous and abstract book that begs to be read again, and even again." *Richard Dayringer, ThD, Professor and Director, Program in Psychosocial Care, Department of Medical Humanities; Professor and Chief, Division of Behavioral Science, Department of Family and Community Medicine, Southern Illinois University School of Medicine*